DATE DUE			
GAYLORD			PRINTED IN U.S.A.

Visit Our Website
www.IssueManagement.org

ISSUE
MANAGEMENT
Origins of the Future

ISSUE MANAGEMENT

Origins of the Future

by
W. HOWARD CHASE

Stamford, Connecticut

Copyright ©1984 by Issue Action Publications, Inc.

All rights reserved.

Issue Action Publications, Inc.
105 Old Long Ridge Road
Stamford, Connecticut 06903

Library of Congress Catalog Card Number: 83-083079

ISBN 0-913869-01-5

First printing: May, 1984

Printed in the United States of America

The
Underlying
Thesis

People who ignore the causal relationships between known trends and predictable events should not be surprised that many will not respect the opinions they hold about the events.

The issue management process, described in this book, is for the person who sees things whole, the reader who is eager and anxious to identify, analyze, and place priorities on trends, and then to exert direct influence on events through issue action programming.

Issue Management

Function: To *manage* both profit and policy by disciplined process—not by visceral impulse.

Objective: To *participate* in formation of public policy that affects an institution, instead of being the end of the crack-the-whip line dominated by external, and usually adversarial forces.

Goal of this Book: To *provide* both the rationale and disciplines for effective issue/policy management.

Contents

Preface

Three major revolutions in the structure of corporate and institutional management have occurred within the last hundred years, and a fourth is under way.

The first of these four significant revolutions came with the invention of double-entry bookkeeping. Gone is the bookkeeper with the green eyeshade and steel-rimmed spectacles sitting on a tall stool at an inclined worktable. Modern debt structures, the capacity to relate equity to debt ratios, validation of common and preferred stock offerings and bonded indebtedness, and most of the apparatus of modern financial management would not have been possible without double-entry bookkeeping. The increasing complexities of modern accounting practices in turn served as a powerful stimulant to the growth of professional management.

Double-Entry Bookkeeping

The second revolution was the shift from owner-management to professional management. As recently as 50 years ago, the corporate landscape was generously endowed with family name corporations: Washburn Crosby, Westinghouse, Baker Chocolate, Studebaker, Durant, and Ford, to name a miniscule fraction. In almost every case, the founders or their heirs were dominant in policy and management.

Shift from Owner- to Professional Management

With growth, complexity, and inheritance tax penalties, plus the frequent fact that the heirs had lost the hunger characteristic of their fathers and grandfathers, or frequently simply weren't up to senior management responsibilities, hired professional managers began to assume the top corporate positions. This trend was discernible early in the 20th century, and today almost all the largest 1,000 companies in America are governed by salaried professional executives. Indeed, it is almost a mark of pride for corporations today to emphasize the fact that "no one owns more than two percent of the stock."

Under owner-managership, there was a certain predictability in both policy and strategy. To a great degree, this quality today is rare. Indeed, today's chief executive generation now has an average job-life expectancy of about six years. Predictable corporate character has changed to predictable impermanence in announced corporate objectives. The buzzword of the CEO today is "restructuring." Sears sells stocks. American Can sells insurance. The old order changes.

The Computer

The computer created the third revolutionary wave. In 1950, there were only about 125 computers in all of American industry. They did exist in elementary form in the military, the Atomic Energy Commission, the National Security Agency, and to even a lesser degree within the FBI and the CIA. With the computer's infinite capacity to accept, store, retrieve and pour out data, the days of the owner-managers were numbered. With only rare exceptions, they could not even understand the languages of the new breed of programmers, much less know how to use their tools. COBOL, BASIC, FORTRAN and other similar code words, more advanced computers with even more complicated symbols and numbers, and other complexities of information systems management, now supervised at vice president or senior vice president levels, left most owner-managers hopelessly at sea.

The fourth revolution is the growing recognition that management of policy is as important as the management of people and profit, that it requires new and teachable skills, and that the disciplines of issue/policy management are vital to corporate and institutional survival in a politicized age.

We now support this thesis.

Policy Management Equal with Profit Management

Acknowledgements

This book is a narrative describing the origins of issue/policy management, by that name, and the author's appraisal of its significance and future. It is relatively uncluttered by footnotes and cross references to the intellectual and professional leadership of a great many contributors to this new management art and science.

To name none of them would be an egregious error. To name all would be an impossibility. With apologies to the many whose names are omitted— each of whom really deserves an entire chapter in recognition of his or her accomplishments—we concentrate on a few conspicuous carriers of the issue/policy management banner.

On the corporate management side, they certainly include Raymond P. Ewing of Allstate, currently chairman of the Issues Management Association; Barry Jones, co-creator of the Issue Management Process Model; Kathleen MacDonough of General Foods; Kerryn King, recently retired from senior vice presidency of Texaco; J. Phillip Halstead of Clorox; Thomas H. Chase of A.T.&.T., Jack W. Hamilton of DuPont; Leonard Harris of the *New York Times*; Jack Rushing of Allied Corporation; Rene Zentner, recently retired from Shell Oil; Margaret Stroup of Monsanto; Erol Caglarcan while at R.J. Reynolds; Michel Curti of Alcan; Pamela S. Diamond of CIGNA; Dawn S. Ford of TVA; Jon C. Holtzman with the Chemical Manufacturers Association; Ronna Klingenberg Lichtenberg of Prudential; Brian C. Milton of Bell Canada; Richard N. Sawaya of Atlantic Richfield; John T. Snow of Sears; Patrick F. Van Keuren of American Can; Carter A. Weiss of J.C. Penney; and many others whom it is an injustice not to mention.

Academia, government, associations, and the attitudinal research fields have furnished many issue management pioneers. They include Walter A. Hahn, formerly of the Congressional Research Service and now professor at George Washington University; Madelyn Hochstein of Yankelovich, Skelly & White and president of the Issues Management Association; David Allnut of Concordia University in Montreal; Walter G. Barlow of Research Strategies Corporation; H. Darden Chambliss of the Aluminum Association; Franck de Chambeau of the American Management Associations; Henry L. Ernstthal of the Society of Nuclear Medicine; Gerald C. Gummersell of Concordia University, Montreal; Ian Wilson of SRI; Kenneth W. Hunter of the U.S. General Accounting Office; Joseph Kenner of New York University's Graduate School of Business; D. Jeffrey Lenn of George Washington University; Dennis Little of the U.S. Library of Congress; George Marotta of the Hoover Institution; Dennis McConnell of the University of Maine; John Crothers Pollock, Jr. of Research & Forecasts, Inc.; Kenneth Schwartz of Opinion Research Corporation; Diana R. Shayon of Human Resources Network; S. Prakash Sethi of Baruch University; and again, many others. Valerie Adams and Agnes McShane over and over transmuted chaotic scribblings into organized sentences, paragraphs, and chapters.

The common denominator of these listed and unlisted leaders is that they found within issue/policy management a new and challenging experience. It provided a sense of enlarged destiny and social usefulness, an orderly response to a disordered world.

I personally thank all of these listed and unlisted men and women for the contributions they have made to my own thinking and to my confidence that the disciplines of issue/policy management are now shaping and will greatly shape the futures of both public and private sectors.

I also thank Teresa Yancey Crane, who helped invent the Issue Management Process Model, and whose company, Issue Action Publications, Inc., had the patience to wait the considerable time it took to write this book, and then the courage to publish it.

Finally, my endless gratitude goes to Elizabeth Coykendall Chase, my wife, who demanded substance where it did not appear, and who censorially but wisely crossed out the derogatory comments, intended and unintended, about traditionalists who do not wish to be disturbed by innovation. Her comment, on reading this paragraph, was, "Well, you got them in anyway, didn't you."

ISSUE
MANAGEMENT
Origins of the Future

Origins of Issue Management

CHAPTER ONE

Evolution From Traditional Practices

"We are perishing for want of wonder,
not for want of wonders."

—*G.K. Chesterton*

Even the term **public issue management** had never appeared in print until April 15, 1976. Each of the three words has always been in the public domain, but the concept of public issue management as a senior executive function, with disciplines acquirable only through training, had origins in the nature of America's pluralistic society itself.

The very term, *private enterprise*, with its implications that the privacy of entrepreneurs was not to be invaded, inhibited application of the "right to know" doctrine until well into the 20th century. For as long as the major functions of federal government were believed to be the insurance of domestic tranquillity, defense against aggressors, and the collection of tariffs, the "right to know" advocates were swimming upstream. Even today, some industrial and financial and even government leaders accept grudgingly the fact that every institution, public or private, is constantly on trial before the bar of public opinion. Still fewer chief executive officers today give more than lip service to the principle that public understanding and acceptance of corporate public policy is at least as important as their full explanation of profit. It simply isn't "cricket," or "good form" to place another value, such as policy, on the pedestal long reserved exclusively for profit. After all, even explanation of size and cause of profit was alien to the private sector three generations ago.

A few brave rebels carried the torch for the public's right to know about profits. **Corporate Public Issues and Their Management (CPI),** on April 1, 1983, discussed their pioneering efforts and the movement they started, and, with some adaptation, the report follows:

Press Relations

"The late Pendleton Dudley, founder of Dudley, Anderson & Yutzy, in 1910 hand-delivered the first corporate financial release ever received by

The Wall Street Journal. His pioneering peers, John Hill, Carl Byoir, 'Tommy' Ross, Sally Woodward, Edward Bernays, Mabel Flanley, and others, each in his or her own way, followed the Dudley example and created the corporate awareness that communication with an observing society is an essential management process.

Public Relations

"The founders of corporate communications through press relations were haunted by their belief that financial press relations was but a first step in a long process. Any perceived validity of Vanderbilt's 'public-be-damned' theory was irreversibly lost. President Roosevelt's 'first hundred days' were conclusive in evidence to all but a few (e.g., Liberty League) that the public insisted upon and endorsed a much broader interrelationship between the public and private sectors.

"The leadership that founded the Public Relations Society of America in 1947-48 generally agreed with this author's definition: 'Public relations is an *operating* philosophy that integrates the corporation into the daily lives of the people it serves.' (This definition was never formally adopted.)

"PRSA, which grew from about 200 members in 1948 to more than 11,000 in 1983, has faithfully represented its members' conviction that total communications must supersede financial communications, and that press relations is but one aspect of a larger role in community relations, consumerism, contribution management, etc.

Public Affairs

"Public affairs, and its principal spokesman, the Public Affairs Council, represented the third stage in a momentous evolution. A growing number of the relationships fraternity concluded that practice of communications in general left a vacuum for a new specialization—the relationships between the public and private sectors. The enormous growth of government as a partner (some called it a dictatorship) in private sector concerns was an exciting lure for new talents.

Issue Management

"In each case, however, the skills listed above tended to be reactive. That is, they have been used primarily to project the values of traditional existing institutions to the public or its government in a communications competition to persuade the public that 'our cause is just.' Thus, other causes must be unjust.

"The newer breed of issue manager began to emerge in 1973. The issue manager believes that a partnership between the private sector and the great social forces demands not only communication, but *participation* in the development of policies which impact an organization.

Policy Management

"This stage is simply a natural evolution. A growing number of chief executive officers have perceived that exclusive preoccupation with profit *now* creates public policy problems that they, in their current organizational forms, are ill-equipped, or not at all equipped, to meet. Strategic planning, confined traditionally to expansion of profit and stimulated by the flood of MBAs, has not diminished policy problems but has rather magnified them. The management of public policy is increasingly perceived at high executive levels to be part and parcel of sound management of profit, now and in the future. Availability of new disciplines for management of profit/policy provided new tools to meet new challenges. Hence, creation of a still newer breed, the issue/policy manager.

Comment

"Each stage of evolution, from financial press releases to policy/profit management, has represented what the poet and author Charles Kingsley in 1874 called 'divine discontent' with what is. It is significant that not one of these evolving groups has ever demeaned the importance of the techniques represented by its precursors. The skills involved in press relations, more generalized public relations, and then public affairs have remained important and are generally appreciated.

"We do not pretend to know where it will end. But of this we are certain: the fighting for turf between champions of any of the evolving stages (and their resultant organizations) is a losing game. Each of the evolving skills is important to all the others. Without tradition, the innovators have nothing against which to rebel. What is emerging, however, is a new and larger vision. Techniques in themselves do not thrill the multitudes nor command support. The larger vision requires the chief executive officer, alone or with aides, to equate public policy with profit and with leadership itself, and to act upon this conviction.

"It is this 'will to act' that separates the genuine executive from the advisors and the trend generalists. John Naisbitt's book, *Megatrends*, seems to say that trends are inexorable and the job of management is to accommodate to them.

"The issue executive recognizes trends, to be sure. But, he/she believes that the private sector is a vital part of our society, and can help create and direct policy, rather than merely react to policy trends established by other forces.

"For the issue manager, history can be created, not just survived."

Change Thanksgiving?

The following is a modest example. In 1939, when none of us had ever heard the term *public relations*, the American Retail Federation planned, organized, and executed the first of two Retailers' National Forums. President Franklin Roosevelt was guest speaker at the Mayflower Hotel in Washington. Flanking him at the speakers' table were five Cabinet members. The retailing giants had a national audience never before achieved. It mattered little (in the long run) that one of its fruits was the proclamation, by Roosevelt, that the traditional Thanksgiving Day would be advanced to the third Thursday of November, rather than the traditional fourth, in order to lengthen the Christmas shopping season.

Public opposition was instantaneous, emotional, and enormous, but Thanksgiving was changed for one year. This demonstrated that business-government cooperation can pre-determine events in behalf of a clearly stated issue—not excluding changing the sacred date of Thanksgiving. This event, fragile and impermanent as it was, clearly established that disciplines were "out there" by which private sector issues could be identified, analyzed, determined to be of high or low priority, and could achieve public policy results through concentrated issue action programming. These conclusions are infinitely clearer in hindsight than they were then.

The experiences of issue management networking with President Roosevelt, "Tommy the Cork" Corcoran, Harry Hopkins and other presidential intimates and advisors demonstrated that a dynamic or pro-active response to a problem that could only be resolved at political levels was both more effective—and more fun!—than negative reaction.

To be precise, the incident dramatized the difference between traditional communications practices and issue action programming. We did, after all, *change* the date of Thanksgiving!

The distinction just drawn between communications as a reflexive or defensive skill, with the primary obligation to portray the company in the best possible light, and issue action, or actually putting the company into the policy-making arena, became the precursor of issue management theory and discipline. The "why" was self-evident, the "how" had to be created.

The introduction of computers into corporations after 1950 had made it both possible and necessary to create systems management applicable to all profit-making functions. The one major function which seemed to be immune to management by process was, or so it seemed to me, that of corporate externalities, generally labelled public relations/public affairs. Line managers, having become accustomed to process, began to refer to the public relations fraternity as the "Chairman's boys and girls," the ultimate insult. The "profession" seemed to be defending yesterday's practices and falling far short of actually shaping policy. Public relations practitioners had at their fingertips an arsenal of communications techniques, but little access to risk assessment or strategic planning processes vital to senior management policy decision-making. Yet no CEO ever hesitated to ask for public relations services to explain policy decisions that he or others had made.

Were we permanently doomed to be "Little Sir Echoes?" Would we ever deserve to be invited to join the policy motivators?

Six years of corporate public affairs officership at American Can, ending in then compulsory retirement in 1975, provided the corporate laboratory in which to explore the answer to that question. William F. May, then corporate CEO and now Dean of New York University's School of Business Administration, liked new ideas and new concepts. True, he and other executives expected maximum "professionalism" in traditional communications, but none interposed obstacles to an attempt to transform external relations capabilities, often visceral in nature, to disciplined process management of issues. Under these hospitable auspices and after innumerable scribblings

The Concept of Process Management

and designs, the Issue Management Process Model (described later) began to take on the form of process, rather than inspiration.

These explorations into the anatomy of change were not altogether popular with old friends. There were growing numbers of bright, able, but traditional external relationists who secretly and sometimes publicly wished that Chase would simply go away. He was rocking a comfortable old boat.

The fourth, or aborning, revolution in management, the systems management of issues and policy, demanded more than an instinct for change or an executive disappointment in traditional public relations.

Issue management demanded first a rationale, then a literature, then adaptation to academic and sound management disciplines. There were obstacles to be overcome, senior managements to be persuaded to use the growing talent available. Towering over even these formidable obstacles was the essentiality of *vision*, the picture in one's mind of what could actually happen when—and if—the private sector became co-equal with government and citizens in the formation of public policy, rather than being the tail of the policy kite flown by others.

Succeeding chapters will deal with these and other travails of issue/policy management in its inevitable emergence as the fourth major management revolution of the past century.

CHAPTER TWO

Early Issue Management Literature

"In this twilight of power,
there is no quick path to
a convenient light switch."

—*Adlai Ewing Stevenson*
Harvard, June 17, 1965

Not to demean the hundreds of books by honored scholars on the social, economic, and political impacts of change upon traditional management practices of the private sector, but with only rare exceptions, the majority of these books made it all too clear that government, aided and abetted by adversarial groups, was in the saddle. The accommodations to the public weal were to be made by corporate structures, certainly not by government, whose perennial growth was regarded by most academicians as a given.

To remain accredited, graduate schools of business administration had to install "modules" into their MBA programs, usually called "Business and Society." Scholars wrote and teachers used any of a half dozen textbooks by the same name.

The more vigorously the professors, authors, and politicians attacked business, the better their books sold, the higher lecture and consultative fees they received, and the more likely "anti-Establishment" politicians were to be elected. Never underestimate the masochistic tendencies of guilt-ridden capitalist managers!

Rising Public Suspicion Toward Private Sector

The rising tides of public suspicion about private sector management had two predictable effects: (1) While in 1950, according to almost every major pollster, about 85 percent of the general public professed respect for private management, by 1980 that figure had sunk to perhaps 15-17 percent. (2) The second predictable result was that companies, increasingly subject to criticism, hired public relations and public affairs practitioners by the thousands to defend them before the court of public opinion. Corporate expenditures of the 1,000 largest companies for public relations in 1950—minus institutional advertising—were in the range of $300 million. By 1980, it was $3 billion. But even this tenfold increase, being largely defensive, did not stop the precipitous decline of public favor or support for the corporate world.

The buzzwords were "Communicate: Tell our side of the story." But since the winds of public wrath were blowing from all quarters, these professional communicators—and their managements—spent most of their time and budgets in monotonous defense in speeches—not action, or in design or color improvements in company literature.

With the initiative almost entirely in the hands of intellectual antagonists of the private sector, and with both print and electronic media as willing reporters of adversarial charges, the "communicators" were constantly being forced into rear-guard action, "protecting the flanks."

The Board of Directors of the American Society of Association Executives demonstrated this Maginot Line approach perfectly as recently as March, 1983. After deliberation, they officially approved a list of "15 major issues facing association management" and recommended strong opposition to each of the 15. Shaping the future through issue/policy management failed to make the agenda.

The Maginot Line Approach

Lacking either theory or practice in working with government as *co-equal* in helping formulate the public policies, corporate chief executive officers fell into a semantic trap. Of course, they didn't mean to. But by 1983 more than 200 companies (of the Fortune 1,000) have formally published their creeds of "Corporate Social Responsibility" and maintain Board-level committees by the same or related names.

But what they had failed to understand was that the *definition* of corporate social responsibility was largely the creature of their adversaries. The problem became how to write such a creed in terms that would be acceptable to the Ralph Naders and the ubiquitous corporate critics.

Consistent with the usual failures of defensive strategies, this one hasn't worked either. Very shortly, Nader, along with his allies, began to denounce the very CEOs who were professing a willingness to accept such social responsibilities. *Who are these people?* Nader asked. *Their very corporate structures are antithetical to the public interest. Why should the public trust them to assume leadership in social decision-making? Who appointed them trustees in behalf of the public interest?*

In short, even the defensive assumption of "corporate social responsibilities" by company after company diminished the impact of anti-private sector attacker by neither jot nor tittle. Nor did it improve corporate reputations, in general, as measured by pollsters.

In the endless contest for a dominant share of the human mind, the once-mighty engine of private, productive enterprise was in a skull-butting contest with the impudent, irreverent, but mighty engines of statism—and was losing the battle. Everywhere.

Millions of words, hundreds of books, thousands of articles and broadcast interviews had turned the competition for public loyalty and appreciation into a Tower of Babel.

"The IMC Letter"

By stretching the imagination, *The IMC Letter,* standing for *Innovation and the Management of Change,* could be construed as early issue management literature. For thirteen years preceding the launching of *Corporate Public Issues and Their Management* (or from 1962-76), this author twice monthly wrote and distributed one of the world's smallest publications.

Yet it represented a concern about the impermanence of status quo and the early birth pangs of the theory and disciplines of issue/policy management.

In 1976, *IMC*, a kind of intellectual moonlighting, blended into *CPI*. From *CPI*'s beginning, it was a symbol of inner turmoil shared by a large number of external relationists. It is sometimes traumatic to shift from being a reflector of what *is*, or seems to be, into an actual participant in the formation of policy.

Despite *IMC* and *CPI*, and the hundreds of books by scholars who described the shortfalls of and challenges facing the private sector, there was a rare unanimity of silence about an escape hatch, or a systems process for doing something about these challenges.

There was no clear voice to announce loudly and clearly that a totally new management science, backed by sturdy disciplines, had to be invented if management retreat from actual contribution to public policy formation were not to become a rout.

CPI nailed the issue management manifesto to the cathedral door in its first issue, April 15, 1976. *CPI*'s objectives were *"to introduce and validate a breakthrough in corporate management design and practice, in order to manage corporate public policy/issues at least as well, or better than the traditional management of profit-center operations.*

"The premise, of course, is that traditional management is in deep trouble with public opinion, and that this fact handicaps corporate effectiveness and even jeopardizes survival in a politicized society....

"It is obvious that a breakthrough in management design and practice cannot leave traditional patterns intact. To scramble an egg, one breaks the shell....

"The thesis and impact of CPI inevitably lead to fundamental revisions of costly, inefficient, and divisive practices of traditional line/staff manage-

"Corporate Public Issues and Their Management" (CPI)

ment. There can be today only one management with one objective: survival and return on capital sufficient to maintain productivity, whatever the economic and political climate."

With profit as the single object of entrepreneurship failing to beguile the multitudes, the new science of issue/policy management was clamoring to be born.

CEO Validation

Two weeks earlier, March 29, 1976, to be precise, *CPI's* thesis had received senior corporate operational validation from William S. Woodside, now American Can's chairman and CEO, in a speech before the Paperboard Packaging Council:

"I, as a manager," he stated, "have two choices. Either I confess to disillusion about any chance of creating a public attitude conducive to the future of our business and to that of all entrepreneurship, or I look for a management process breakthrough, a new type of systems management that can be practically adapted to the public issues that confront us.

"What kind of a management system can corporate executives devise to prevent single and coordinated anti-establishment issue protagonists from overwhelming us through their sheer emotional power to turn the passive middle into activist foes?

"The conclusion in our company is that *we must concentrate on single issue management, with all the energy we use on product market development and acceptance.* To do this requires profound organizational change, which we are tackling."

Thus, in a single month, both a publication and a major corporate executive had introduced the dynamic concept of issue management into the literature and practice of senior management.

A Rising Tide

In succeeding months and years, and to this day, *CPI* has combed past and present literature for examples of issue management. Sources ranged from Sun Tzu's *Art of War*, written 2,500 years ago, to examples from companies, unions, foundations, and governments of evolving application of issue/policy management at work. As early as 1976, CPI called attention to SmithKline's publication program called "Issues for Action." Although the term "networking" had not yet entered the external affairs language, the Public Affairs Council in 1976, began its "public interest profiles" of activist groups with their varying demands for reform of the corporate system. While this could not be called issue management literature, it was representative of the issue-consciousness-raising trend.

In fact, a great welter of ideas and activities related to public issues, but under a galaxy of labels, seemed to have been galvanized by *CPI*'s creation of a name, *issue management*. Within a single year after the name appeared, issue management was firmly established, sometimes as a desirable innovation and sometimes as a target for semantic dispute.

The Public Affairs Council began the first of its series of seminars on issue management in 1977, with this writer as the first proponent. Within two years, at least 50 consulting firms were letter-heading issue management as one of their special services. Ponderous articles appeared condemning issue management on the charge that issues "couldn't be managed—only responded to," or, in any event, the title was "manipulative," and would therefore be suspect, "especially by the media."

Then, too, there were spates of articles and books which almost grudgingly adopted the semantics of issue management, but not the disciplines. Almost invariably, these critics pronounced that issue management was merely a new name for traditional practices. Few indicated that past methods weren't working to bridge the chasm between business and society.

Peter Drucker's definition of management comes to the rescue: *"Management,"* he wrote, *"is the art of achieving results through others."* Further reflection makes it clear that there is no action taken by corporate management, by government, religious leaders, or educators which is not intended to be persuasive or "manipulative."

Of greater importance than the contemporary debates about the substance and relevance of issue management—debates that frequently took on caterwauling intensity—was the fact that both friend and foe were arguing their cases from a quicksand of literary inadequacy.

There was, in fact, still no basic literature on issue management which defined its attendant disciplines. One of the root causes of violent arguments about the subject was the absence of a basic, hardrock definition. Until such a base could be established, founded on scholarship and research, all issue management discussions were foredoomed to be tinny.

A Process Design

My then-colleague, Barry Jones, and I set out to try to fill this vacuum. If issue management were truly a new management discipline, then that discipline demanded a diagrammatic model. None existed. And until there was a model, there could be, and were, torrents of words, but no system or structure. Barry, his brilliant colleague, Teresa Yancey Crane, and I sat on a lot of floors surrounded with poster paper, inventing the **Chase/ Jones Issue Management Process Model.** Just as the computer had made process management possible for production, marketing, and finance, we sought a legitimate process by which traditional public relations and public affairs practitioners could be transformed into dynamic policy makers, rather than remain yesterday's reactive policy reflectors. We sought what previously had been an impossible dream: systems management of issues and policy.

The Model in its entirety appears in Section II, Chapter 3. Each of the four segments of the Model will reappear in chapter form as we discuss the consecutive process involved.

The Issue Management Process

"Discipline," says *Webster's New Collegiate Dictionary*, "is a branch of knowledge involving research...; training which corrects, molds, strengthens, or perfects...; a rule or system of rules affecting conduct or action...; practical rules as distinguished from dogmatic formulations."

This Section is an attempt to provide the *disciplines* of issue management in contrast to the frequent welter of visceral techniques which are standard practice for traditional public relations/public affairs practitioners.

It is an attempt to create a frame of reference in which all these useful techniques of communication can have a larger social utility—and respect—than they now "enjoy."

CHAPTER THREE

The Process Model For Issue Management

"Originality is the result of
combining things across disciplines."

—*Thomas Gold*
Astronomer, Cornell University

As so often happens to proud inventors, the world did not proceed to build a highway to the issue management door. Daring to imply that the management of public policy is as important as the management of profit was considered heresy for some.

But the University of Maryland, more tolerant or more innovative, printed "Managing Public Policy Issues," in its Summer, 1979, *Public Relations Review.* We reproduce it here, with a few modifications. It is the seminal beginning of the literature of issue management.

"Managing Public Policy Issues"

Despite the billions of dollars companies and their associations have spent on "external relations" (public relations, public affairs, government relations, communications, etc.), business in general has been ineffective in defining and then validating its position on public policy issues.

Explanations or excuses are plentiful. The most significant explanation of the failure of business to gain respect for its positions on public issues is that corporate leadership either does not recognize, or ignores, the discernible trends which always precede emerging issues. (In either event, it is obviously impossible to manage issues which are the predictable results of unforeseen trends.)

Since the significant introduction of the computer into business (around 1950), professionally-trained management has devised systems for the major profit-center functions (finance, production, marketing, etc.), but has failed to apply a disciplined systems process to public issue and to public policy management. When challenged by today's activism, business tends to react to overt symptoms, rather than to identify and analyze fundamental causes of the trend which has led to a critical issue.

It is not surprising, then, that when a critical

"FRIGHT WIG ARTISTS"

Before issue management and legislative track-ing deserved the title of disciplines, one vice president and Washington representative of a large company identified his Washington col-leagues and himself as "fright wig artists." The route, he said, to a larger salary, a new rug, a new carafe, was to call the CEO on Monday morning, just ahead of the weekly senior man-agement meeting, and to say that "All hell has broken loose down here. Senator X has just introduced a bill we can't live with."

He told me one day that his boss never once asked him why he hadn't been networking with Senator X's aides while the bill was in its mark-up stage.

---

issue reaches the public policy decision-making point, business finds itself defendant in the court of public opinion. Since CEOs have had no sys-tems methodology governing the issue manage-ment process (until now), all too often they turn to outworn and traditional public relations defense mechanisms. When Churchill announced that he had not become the King's First Minister "to preside over the liquidation of the British Empire," that is precisely what he did do. Sim-ilarly, it seems quixotic to turn to methods—and to people—under whose public affairs supervision public trust of the business structure has plum-meted from about 75 per cent to 18 per cent between 1950 and 1978.

And when business loses its trial before the court of public opinion, it is usually forced to accept costly legislative, regulatory, administra-tive, or judicial verdicts that severely inhibit the entrepreneurial decision-making function at the cost of loss of productivity.

The major thesis developed here is that *issue management can now be as much a systems process as the management of profit centers.* Our subthesis is that we have no hesitation in speaking about corporate public policy management. Public policy is *not* the exclusive domain of government. In our pluralistic society, public policy is the result of interaction between public and private points of view. The corporation, as an institution, has every moral and legal right to participate in *formation* of public policy—not merely to react, or be responsive, to policies designed by government.

Background for Issue Management Thesis

Erosion of public support handicaps all levels of corporate operations and jeopardizes survival in a politicized economy. As Yankelovich, Skelly and White write: "Senior corporate management must understand that government intervention which affects the bottom line is strongly supported by the public, and for this reason is not likely to diminish in the foreseeable future—indeed, it may increase significantly. Therefore, one must communicate to management that the anticipation of and response to public policy requires a

---

CITIZEN, BUSINESS, GOVERNMENT INTERACTION

The three overlapping circles at the heart of each stage of the Model, labelled Citizens, Business, and Government, illustrate this point. None of the three, by itself, makes public policy. Policy is the end result of their interaction. The effectiveness of Business, for example, in contributing to the end product—public policy—depends on the skill with which it understands and uses the issue management process, by whatever name.

long-term institutionalization of a new function which identifies issues early and allows sufficient time for analysis and corporate response."[1]

Why should business identify and respond to accelerating social, economic, and political changes? Sixty-eight leaders of business, labor, professions, civic organizations, and governments debated this question at a Spring, 1978, conference on corporate governance, sponsored by the American Assembly, a nonpartisan forum founded by Dwight D. Eisenhower, while president of Columbia University.

Assembly participants agreed that the corporation has been a vehicle for unparalleled prosperity, but, like other institutions, it must adapt to the times. They also agreed that management, which often lags in recognizing the significance of emerging issues, should increase efforts to anticipate social change and to respond to reasonable public expectations. These efforts are necessary for two reasons. First, society is asking whether material progress is enough, whether private enterprises, especially large public corporations, should not also be expected to fulfill a complex mix of social goals.

Second, relatively new corporate stakeholders are demanding action on issues such as environmental protection, community renewal, corporate influence overseas, energy conservation, and employment of women and minorities. These new stakeholders (consumers, employees, and the community) want the resources and economic power of the corporation used to build a better society.

Management, the Assembly decided, must respond to the needs and expectations of stakeholders, as well as stockholders, *because social*

---

[1] *Incorporating Social and Political Analysis into Business Decision-Making* (New York: Yankelovich, Skelly and White, Inc., 1978), p. 13.

responsibility and profit are compatible. The Assembly, including its 16 business members, recommended that trade associations and corporate boards have a primary role in interpreting public concerns and emerging demands to management, which then should develop a public issue evaluation system. This system should be a professional resource for monitoring executive decision-making and actions on public concerns. It should also measure the performance of middle and lower management by the public policy consequences of their operations.[2]

Evidence grows that corporate governance is far more flexible and adaptable than state or national governance which establishes the rules for corporate forces. It must be so in order to survive. The overwhelmingly important challenge faced by professional senior management is how to develop and establish a systems approach to the management of public policy issues in order not to surrender corporate autonomy and efficiency to the whims or specialized pressures of bureaucrats and activist groups.

Establishing a systems process for the management of public policy issues is an achievable goal. It is consistent with management systems and techniques used in traditional profit-center operations. In fact, ever since Henri Fayol, father of the process school of management, refined the concept of long-range planning, and Alfred G. Sloan helped invent the modern corporation, business organizations have moved steadily toward systematization (in almost every phase of profit management, but with little progress toward policy management).

Today, most corporations use strategic plan-

---

[2]*Corporate Governance in America* (Harriman, NY: The American Assembly and Columbia University, 1978), pp. 4-10.

EXECUTIVE SOUL-SEARCHING

This kind of reevaluation of the corporate role in a dynamic society is characteristic of an inordinate amount of business executive soul-searching. It appears again and again under the auspices of the Committee for Economic Development, the Conference Board, the national Chamber of Commerce, the National Association of Manufacturers, and Cooperative Business-Education Forums, to name only a few hosts for these consciousness-raising discussions.

Their shortfall, however, lies in the fact that diagnosis, however accurate, is of little value without an issue process and an issue action program to *do* something about the perceived needs.

---

ning systems to organize and coordinate management of the "four M's"—money, machines, marketing and men/women. But only recently have some corporations (e.g., Sun, Crown Zellerbach, General Electric, Texaco, Northwestern Bell, Consumers Power, CNA, United Telecommunications, Sperry, and Rexnord) taken steps toward the application of a systems process to improve their effectiveness in the competiton for the *minds* of people, a vital "fifth M" in corporate systems planning.

Success or failure in this competition for public support can be demonstrated to have as much, if not more, impact on corporate productivity and profitability as the management of finance, production, marketing, and personnel. But sound public policy management must start at home—within the corporate structure. John D. Harper, as Alcoa's chairman, has written:

When the manager sets out to relate with the society, it is not necessary to go into the inner city or to city hall or to Washington or to any distant place. The central corporate relationship with society occurs within the corporate wall; virtually every corporate decision and practice; every contact with shareholders, employees, suppliers and customers, ultimately has effect upon society and upon the corporation's standing in the society's esteem and respect. This is an important perspective...if we are to keep the corporation in step with our changing society.[3]

Many corporate leaders recognize that their actions or inactions affect the well-being of mankind and that their philosophy, as well as performance, is of proper public interest. For example, at the Sun Company, the Board of Directors has adopted a creed or statement of principles to guide its policies and practices. These principles or Board-accepted truths require the establishment of public policy management at the highest level of executive responsibility. Three of Sun's principles in particular illustrate the need for public policy management within every corporation. Sun believes that such management must:

- "nourish societal values, as well as perform profitably;
- "conduct its affairs responsibly; and
- "respect the needs and aspirations of others while seeking their understanding of the policies and practices of the company."

(Again, the goals are noteworthy. The "how-to-achieve-them" does not appear.)

In the words of David Rockefeller, as chairman of Chase Manhattan Bank:

Participation in public policy is both a basic responsibility of corporate executives and a management function which, like any other, must be approached with systematic business discipline. Corporations must establish public policy objectives, set priorities, imple-

---

[3]John D. Harper, "The Changing Manager," *Management Awareness*, Vol. 4, No. 1 (1978), p. 81.

ment a working plan and set guidelines for measuring their success. In the world of today, the diverse activities we call government and public relations, lobbying and issue advertising, must all be part of an integrated management strategy.[4]

(In other words, Rockefeller anticipates the Issue Management Process.)

But these examples demonstrate only that certain thoughtful leaders are describing the need for a "breakthrough in corporate design and practice in order to manage corporate public policy issues at least as well or better than profit-center operations."

The next four chapters represent the process by which the need can be met.

---

[4]David Rockefeller, "Free Trade in Ideas," at The Wharton School, Philadelphia, PA, Jan. 19, 1978.

CHAPTER FOUR

How The Issue/Policy Management Model Works

"Truth *happens* to an idea. It *becomes* true, made true by events. Its verity is in fact an event, a process: the process namely of verifying itself, its veri-*fication*. Its validity is the process of its valid-*ation*."

—*William James*
Pragmatism *(1907)*

The Chase/Jones Issue Management Process Model offers senior executives a resource for integrating diverse line and staff functions into a systems process for public policy management. Use of this Model incorporates public policy planning into every operational unit of the companies which adopt it. The Model increases in sophistication with real-world experience; actual corporate application—in examples to be cited—has already resulted in considerable refinement to meet the realities of individual organizational structures and management styles.

The Model is best described by what it represents. First, it embodies a results-oriented philosophy of management, combining solid management technique with the growing knowledge available from the social, political, and communication sciences. It guides the anticipation and management of change, based on both theoretical observation and practical experience. The Model identifies the significant aspects of public policy decision-making and directs attention away from irrelevant variables or unimportant circumstances. It focuses on the root causes and effects of these decisions.

The Model as a Tool

The Issue Management Process Model is a tool for predicting the effect of internal and external environmental changes on the performance of the overall corporate system. This tool assigns decision-making authority and performance responsibility, and makes possible an objective review and evaluation of issue manager performance.

Second, the Model represents a systems approach, consistent with IBM's Management Business System as it is applied to the management of profit-center operations. Every system is composed of interrelated and interdependent institutions, activities, and values, which are systems in themselves. The Model integrates the functions, processes, and interactions of these subsystems.

As Cleland and King say in *Management: A Systems Approach,* the output from one subsystem is simply the input to another subsystem. Other exchanges occur among the subsystems and between the system and the larger environment in which it operates.

Third, the Model provides a template for the process necessary to integrate various systems, which by concept are static in the sense that they don't move independently. The process is the (totality of) dynamic actions or operations, described in the Model, which propel the overall system.

To understand the dynamics of the issue management process, imagine the Model as a pond, and public policy issues as stones. When a stone drops into a pond, ripples move outward and form concentric circles. When an issue is dropped in the public policy process, at the heart of the Model, the resulting ripples disturb the smooth functioning of (traditional) business practices. How great these disruptions will be depend on their size, number, and how they interact with each other to affect public policy decisions.

The Heart of the Process

Within the public policy process are three decision-making groups: **citizens, business,** and **government.** No one of these groups makes public policy decisions independently. They are interrelated and interdependent. Like the pond, they are elements of a larger ecosystem. They are influenced by the actions or inactions of each other, by those of institutions such as the church, family, labor unions, media, and educational establishments, and by the individual and institutional values supporting an even larger environmental system.

As one element of this larger system, business must respond to forces in the public policy environment. *The predicament facing business today is whether it can act in a manner accepta-*

ble to citizens and government. One encompassing definition of public policy is simply that it is whatever the people and their governments finally do—or do not do.

Who sets the government agenda? Activist groups most often set the public policy agenda by combining propaganda techniques with computer-age technology. First, they create a perceived need for their reform idea in both special-interest and establishment press and before forums of intellectual or opinion leader audiences. Second, they create the appearance of legitimacy for the idea through studies, third-party validation, and ultimately through public referenda or government decisions in bellwether nations, states, or communities. Then, they further employ organizational development, direct mail, and other techniques to broaden their constituency and to extend their idea across this nation and other industrialized societies.

Politically astute activists demand that business leaders change the way they do business. In the face of such challenges, a CEO is left with two choices: inaction or action. If the boss doesn't act, adversaries will.

If the leader does act, the Chase/Jones Issue Management Process Model provides five steps to manage public policy issues systematically. These steps are diagrammed as a series of concentric circles. They are:

1. **Issue Identification,**
2. **Issue Analysis,**
3. **Issue Change Strategy Options,**
4. **Issue Action Programming, and**
5. **Evaluation of Results.**

Again, the public policy process is at the heart of the Model and each of its five steps. The circles that emanate from this central process as rings and subrings show the order, interaction, and progression within each step.

CHAPTER FIVE

Issue Identification

"This sense of identity provides the ability to experience one's self as something that has continuity and sameness, and to act accordingly."

—Erik Homburger Eriksson
Childhood and Society *(1950)*

Accelerating Social, Economic and Political Changes

The adversaries of the modern corporation may be skillful in setting the public policy agenda, but issues do not evolve overnight. *Issue Identification* starts with consideration of trends, which precede issues.

Accelerating Social, Economic, and Political Changes, the first ring in this step, includes 13 illustrative trends that may coalesce into specific issues. *An issue is an unsettled matter which is ready for decision. Trends, on the other hand, are detectable changes which precede issues.*

Resources for Trend Identification

The Model allows for both quantitative and qualitative study of the future. In fact, many corporations maintain futurist experts and departments for the exclusive purpose of studying and reporting on trends. They are using scenarios, extrapolations, cross-impact matrices, Delphi polls, models, games, simulations, and other methodologies to forecast the impact of change on their organizations. General Electric, General Mills, Prudential, the Sun Company, General Telephone and Electronics, and Ford Motor Company—to name only a few—have all conducted studies of trends which may affect the future of their business. Private organizations (e.g., the Hudson Institute), government (e.g., the White House), professional societies (e.g., the World Future Society), and individuals (e.g., Alvin Toffler, Graham Molitor, Glenn T. Seaborg, and Isaac Asimov) are also conducting and publishing studies of the future. Each and every one of these studies is a resource for the corporation that wants to look at the future business environment but is not ready to establish its own "futures" department as an early step in the issue management process.

Any one or a combination of these futurist methodologies and sources aids the manager of corporate public policy. They: **(1)** provide useful frameworks for decision-making and planning;

(2) identify future dangers and opportunities; **(3)** suggest a variety of possible approaches to solving a problem; **(4)** help assess alternative policies and action; **(5)** enable people to see the present more clearly; and **(6)** increase the degree of choice.[1]

Basic Corporate Goal

If the corporation doesn't take advantage of futuristics, it may find itself unprepared to face issues that later invite adverse public policy decisions. These decisions can handicap corporate effectiveness and jeopardize future survival and return on investment—the **Basic Corporate Goal** in the second ring of Issue Identification.

Primary Identification of Specific Issues

No company can simultaneously manage every issue. Therefore, companies need to develop procedures for identifying and sorting out the issues of primary concern to their current operations (explained by **Primary Identification of Specific Issues,** the last ring in this step).

Dr. Robert Moore, as emerging issues coordinator for The Conference Board, has listed seven different procedures for identifying issues. These procedures are:

(1) "Designation by the chief executive officer;

(2) "Informal discussions among senior executives;

(3) "Structured polling of senior executives;

(4) "Selection by a staff unit for senior management consideration and refinement;

(5) "Identification by division or profit-center managers;

(6) "Formal exploratory planning beyond the typical limits of corporate strategic planning; and

(7) "Scanning by staff volunteers of a wide variety of publications."

---

[1]Edward Cornish, *The Study of the Future* (Washington, DC: The World Future Society, 1977), pp. 220-221.

Regardless of the procedure used, the primary goal and objective of the Issue Identification step is to place *initial* priorities on emerging issues. They can be classified by:

- type (social, economic, political, technological);
- impact and response source (business system, industry, corporation, subsidiary, department);
- geography (international, national, regional, state, local);
- span of control (noncontrollable, semicontrollable, controllable); and
- salience (immediacy, prominence).

At this stage, the wheat is separated from the chaff. Each issue emerging from Issue Identification will undergo, separately, the last four steps on the Model. And the corporate response to each issue can be managed with the same expectation of effectiveness as for any other systematized line or staff operation of the corporation.

THE ALCOA EXAMPLE

Jon Holtzman, then at Alcoa and now at Chemical Manufacturer's Association, applied process to issue management, broadening it from the board room, to the entire management of Alcoa, down to foreman level.

After networking with leaders of a dozen activist, governmental, and academic groups, he identified about 150 unduplicated issues which, upon analysis, grouped themselves into 13 general issue categories.

Holtzman, with CEO approval, asked several thousand employees to underline "the ten top issues you believe corporate management should concentrate its attention on over the next few years, because of potential impact on Alcoa and on your operation." He asked for asterisks on each of the top three.

The entire list appeared in *Corporate Public Issues and Their Management (CPI)* in its issue of July 15, 1982.

In May, 1982, the Office of Technology Assessment published its list of 40 major issues facing America, reported in *CPI* for June 1, 1982. The two lists, regardless of source, show remarkable consistency.

In the nation's first MBA course on Issue Management, one issue identification approach always stimulated enthusiastic reaction. Each student was asked to clip daily from papers and magazines, news stories about issues they perceived would affect *their* companies and *their* careers. In a few weeks, without exception, every student had an "Issue Action File" on at least 50 issues.

It was suggested that each student could very well be the only person in the company (all were already corporate employees) to be able—in a few minutes—to discuss with his or her boss and colleagues the background of issues that affect them and their company. To this day, former students are articulately grateful for this issue identification tool.

CHAPTER SIX

Issue Analysis

"Mankind will possess incalculable advantages and extraordinary control over human behavior when the scientific investigator will be able to subject his fellow men to the same external analysis he would employ for any natural object, and when the human mind will contemplate itself not from within but from without."

—*Ivan Petrovich Pavlov*
Bequest to the Academic Youth
of Soviet Russia *(1936)*

Theory and Research

After Issue Identification, those issues of most importance to the corporation are then subjected to **Theory and Research** in the second step of the model, *Issue Analysis*.

Major Sources of Accelerating Change Relevant to the Issue

Again the Model starts from the public policy process at the center. The first task of Issue Analysis is to determine the origin of the issue. The first ring, **Major Sources of Accelerating Change Relevant to the Issue,** lists three generic sources of ferment: the **Social, Economic,** and **Political** trends, forces, and events which affect the public policy process.

Few issues evolve neatly from one source. The controversial issue of roadside litter is a good illustration. The social concerns of environmentalist leaders have evolved into a full-blown political issue, culminating in "bottle bill" legislation with what industry leaders call disruptive economic consequences. Major changes fueling the "bottle bill" issue include fluctuating social and ethical values, the limits-to-growth and quality-of-life movements, energy concerns, the growth of pluralistic politics, and inflation. Sociologist Daniel Bell has characterized the impact of such accelerating change on the business community: "The corporation operates in a social and political context in which it has to be responsive to external issues. In fact, one can say that that which is social today becomes political tomorrow, and economic (in costs and consequences) the day after."[1] (The "bottle bill" example is more explicitly discussed in Stage 3 of the Model, "Issue Change Strategy Options.")

---

[1]Daniel Bell, "Dilemmas of Managerial Legitimacy," at the First National Conference on Business Ethics at Bentley College, Waltham, MA, March 11-12, 1977.

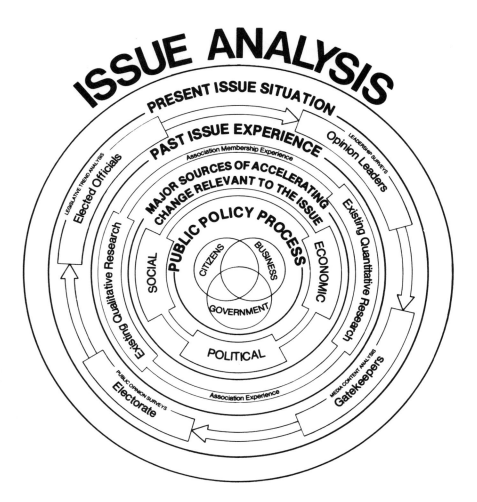

**Past
Issue
Experience**

Since no practical business manager can manage issues that are isolated from the real world, the issue analysis arising from relevant social, economic, and political changes must be measured against **Past Issue Experience.** Within this ring are two large boxes, labelled **Existing Qualitative Research** and **Existing Quantitative Research,** connected by narrow bands containing the words, **Internal Experience** and **External Experience.** Here existing knowledge of the issue is compiled and put into useful form. If the organization has had success or failure in managing an issue, the reasons for that past performance should be collected and reviewed in their raw form (qualitative) and, if necessary, subjected to more rigorous analysis (quantitative). This knowledge may come from within the organization (internal experience) or from other sources beyond the corporation's own resources (external experience).

Existing **Quantitative Research** is the easier of these two types to describe. It consists simply of data that have been analyzed. External sources of quantitative research include opinion polls conducted and published by Yankelovich, Skelly and White, Inc., Cambridge Survey Reports, Opinion Research Corporation, etc., and other types of studies by "think tanks" such as Arthur D. Little, Research Strategies Corporation, and the American Enterprise Institute. If the corporation is a national one, internal quantitative sources may include data from states or localities where public policy decisions have been made, and information collected and quantified on the causes and effects of these decisions.

Existing **Qualitative Research** is used in the form in which it was collected. External sources include reviews of periodical literature to determine what influential leaders and publications are saying about the issue. Internally, qualitative

---

"HOW NICE!"

The pollsters mentioned here, including Walter G. Barlow, president of Research Strategies Corporation and formerly president of Opinion Research Corporation, have notably contributed to executive consciousness-raising about the vital importance of economic, political, and social trends upon business situations.

Most of the attitudinal research leaders, however, have a common lament. After an authorized research study is completed, it is usually presented to an executive group, with multiple visual and sound aids.

The audience is prone to nod appreciatively, say "Isn't that interesting?" and applaud. Then the report is filed, all too often never to be referred to again.

The problem is that, in the absence of a complete process approach to issue management, the quantitative and attitudinal research, furnished at considerable cost, is not always used as a fundamental basis for ultimate issue action programming.

---

research could draw on the experience of employees and associations.

At this point, in the analysis of an issue, the manager should have a fairly clear idea of its origins and evolution. By analyzing the accelerating sources of change along with the existing studies, polls, and experiences relevant to the issue, the issue analyst should now be able to refine further the issue and its impact on the organization. This pragmatic refinement is necessary to avoid expensive waste in the next ring of analysis, Present Issue Situation.

Present Issue Situation

No organization should conduct more original objective research than it needs. However, if existing research is inadequate, the **Present Issue Situation** analysis determines precisely the current intensity of the issue in the public policy process. It demands applied research about the relationship of the issue to the corporation. The four boxes within the ring list, in bold print, those groups which have the most to say in the diffusion of an idea or reformist demand, from **Opinion Leaders,** to mass media **Gatekeepers,** to public opinion held by the **Electorate,** who influence the decision-making of **Elected and Other Government Officials.** In fine print are the means or methodologies of determining the priority of the issue in the estimation of each group. On any given issue, not all four methods (leadership surveys, media content analyses, public opinion surveys, and legislative trend analyses) may be necessary to develop adequate information for making judgments and setting corporate priorities on the issue. However, as is true in any systems process, to ignore any part may represent a perilous complacency.

The first methodology, **Surveys of Opinion Leaders,** reveals some of the most cogent insights. Opinion leaders in a community, state or nation are those who have the stature, awarded by followers because of their visibility or competence, to influence attitudes or overt behavior in a desired way with relative frequency.[2] Categories of opinion leaders selected for interviewing include persons from public interest groups, politics, business, labor, law, or the church. These leaders

---

[2]Everett M. Rogers, et al., "Mass Media and Interpersonal Communication," *Handbook of Communication,* ed. Ithiel de Sola Pool and Wilbur Schramm, et al. (Chicago: Rand McNally College Publishing Co., 1973), pp. 296-299.

are extremely effective in setting the mass media agenda on high-priority policy issues. They create the messages, the media transmit them, and public opinion, as we shall see, is significantly influenced.

The **Media Content Analysis** studies the patterns of newspaper and magazine coverage on any given issue. (Author John Naisbitt has capitalized on this in *Megatrends.*) Defined more fully, "Content analysis is a phase of information-processing in which communication content is transformed, through objective and systematic application of categorization rules, into data that can be summarized and compared."[3]

Data collected can be analyzed and cross-tabulated by a computer-assisted program according to any number of relevant criteria. Barry Jones has conducted a media content analysis for a coalition of seven national trade associations based on these five criteria: (1) the source of the statement; (2) the intent of the statement; (3) the target of the item; (4) the theme or message; and (5) the tactic of which it is a part, or which it represents. The purpose of this particular analysis was to seek objective information on how the media gatekeepers were communicating the issue of restrictive container legislation through the news and editorial columns.

According to Maxwell McCombs, the mass media do not tell people what to think; they tell people what to think about.[4] That is, the media determine which issues—and which organizations—will be put on the public agenda for discus-

---

[3]W.J. Paisley in *Content Analysis for the Social Sciences and Humanities,* Ole R. Holsti (Reading, MA: Addison-Wesley Publishing Co., 1969), p. 3.

[4]Maxwell McCombs, "Agenda-Setting Function of Mass Media," *Public Relations Review,* Vol. 3, No. 4 (Fall 1977), p. 90.

"PAST IS PROLOGUE"

The amazing success of John Naisbitt's book *Megatrends,* mentioned above, is due in large part to his skill in emphasizing the media agenda-setting function.

---

sion. This is called the media agenda-setting function, and its importance cannot be overstated.

Consideration of **Public Opinion** usually focuses on the distribution of opinions pro and con once an issue is before the public. Agenda-setting directs our attention to an earlier stage in the public opinion process, the stage at which an issue emerges. At this point of initial emergence and opinion formation, policymakers and planners still have numerous options at hand. Once an issue is highly salient and opinions are largely shaped, public relations may be limited to a defensive posture or a redundant "me too-ism." Effective public relations as an issue management tool requires lead time and opportunities to communicate before an issue is approaching its zenith. Knowledge of the agenda-setting process and its role in the formation of public opinion can provide these opportunities for effective public relations at the time issues are first emerging on the public agenda.

Applied field research validates the effectiveness with which the opinion leaders use the mass media gatekeepers to set the public policy agenda and influence the formulation of public opinion. There is a positive correlation between what is printed in the newspaper and what people think. Virginia Commonwealth University Professor Tex Auh used a computer-assisted analysis to compare published opinion (media content) with public opinion on the "bottle bill" in Connecticut. There was a positive rank order correlation to the

---

ACTIVIST GROUP INDEX

The Public Affairs Council is performing yeoman service on issues emerging on the public agenda through its periodic review of the anatomy and purpose of activist groups. Called *Public Interest Profiles*, the review divides agenda-setting activist groups into the following categories: Civil Rights, Corporate Accountability, Economic System, Energy, Environment, Governmental Accountability, Legal, Media, and Political Process.

A.T.&T. was one of the first major companies to set operational standards for emerging issues analysis, doing this in August, 1979. Issues considered were: Consumer Privacy, Consumerism, Grey Power, Employee Privacy, and Economics. *However, so rapid has been the speed of change that even in 1979 the potential dismemberment of the company was not considered an issue.*

91st percentile between published and public opinion, statistically valid for the sample sizes involved.

Public opinion surveys of the electorate are like a photograph; they freeze today's reality in time, making it available for later reflection. These data are accurate, although they soon become dated. Public opinion surveys should be used when needed, but not unless the sponsor has a clear idea of what he or she wants to find out. Like the other Issue Analysis methodologies, public opinion surveys have both advantages and limitations. For example, public opinion surveys measure the degree of public acceptance of the corporate or institutional point of view, but they do not measure consensus understanding, accuracy, and congruency between a corporation and its publics on issues of mutual interest. These indicators can be measured, as a supplement to public opinion findings, with another methodology, coorientational analysis.

Public opinion does not have a one-to-one relationship with the action of elected officials. In the words of V.O. Key, Jr.: "To note that opinion on many issues is restricted to small sectors of the population is not to assert that these small blocs of popular opinion are, or may be, ignored by government.... One of the major problems of popular government consists in the determination of when to yield, and when not to yield, to their demands."[5] Thus, the utility of **Legislative Trend Analysis** is to determine the predisposition of elected officials to vote one way or another on a particular issue.

Although company lobbyists can provide a reasonably accurate accounting of how various legislators are likely to vote on a given bill, two other reliable methods of legislative trend analysis can also be used. The first is the anti-industry ranking system developed by public interest groups as a scorecard of how legislators have voted in the past. While this ranking is statistically valid, voting behavior path analysis can also be used. Up to 200 variables can be fed into a computer-assisted program to reveal direct and indirect effects on legislators, the relative contribution of each effect, and whether one variable influences another positively or negatively, and to what extent.

Judgment and Priority Setting

Combining legislative trend analyses with the other three methodologies to analyze the present issue situation, the manager will have scientific data detailing corporate strengths and weaknesses on the issue. Deciding what action to

---

[5]V.O. Key, Jr., *Public Opinion and American Democracy* (New York: Alfred A. Knopf, 1968), p. 92.

take—based on these data and information from past issue experience—requires **Judgment and Priority Setting.** The use of qualitative judgment and quantitative decision-making science will help set priorities among the issues and will help select the most feasible and practical response to individual issues.

CHAPTER SEVEN

Issue Change Strategy Options

"The heavens themselves, the planet,
  and this center,
 Observe degree, priority, and place;
 Insisture, course, proportion, season,
  form,
 Office, and custom, in all line of
  order."

—William Shakespeare
Troilus and Cressida, *I, iii, 85*

Selection among alternatives takes place within the third step of the model, labelled **Issue Change Strategy Options** (more simply, priority setting). Here, basic decisions are made on the corporation's response to challenges or opportunities posed by any one issue within the public policy process. An issue change strategy option is a choice among carefully selected methods and plans for achieving long-term corporate goals in the face of public policy issues, a choice based on the expected effect of each method of employment, cost, sales, and profits. In selecting an issue change strategy option, or priority, an organization decides whether or not to fight, on what battlefield, and when.

Organizations have reason to feel uncertain about their self-direction in the face of rapidly accelerating social, economic, and political changes. The *management of change* is the critical function which must be maintained both within the existing corporate structure and in the public policy arena. Executives must choose between directing or *not* directing change. If they do not manage change, the corporation will lose self-direction, and the possibility of becoming a victim of other-directed change will increase significantly.

However, there are alternatives to being a victim of change. These options are represented by the **Reactive, Adaptive,** and **Dynamic** rings. Choices here are not mutually exclusive, and do not indicate value judgments about the change strategy option chosen. They are only "good or bad" depending on how well they work.[1]

---

[1]The pioneering development and influence of Douglas C. Basil and Curtis W. Cook's "Progressive States of Organizational Characteristics," in *The Management of Change* is acknowledged.

Reactive

The **Reactive** change strategy can be summed up when management says, "Let's stonewall this issue." This strategy represents a continuation of past behavior, in that the organization is reactive to the initiatives of interest groups as well as elected and appointed officials. Using this strategy, the organization attempts to postpone public policy decisions with tactical maneuvers. This is sometimes acceptable, but more often this delaying game leaves little time for legislative, regulatory, administrative, or judicial compromises, and the organization itself can become a victim of change. Ian Wilson, while at General Electric, illustrated this strategy by the "perceived failure of business to deal adequately with the conflicting claims of the energy crisis and a clean environment."[2] This led to party platform planks and bills to control business growth and investment, and to restructure major industries.

Adaptive

The **Adaptive** strategy implies an openness to change, a recognition of its inevitability. It relies on planning as a tool to anticipate change and to offer an accommodation, within or outside formal adversary proceedings, before unacceptable reformist demands are legislated or mandated into public policy. The work of Virginians for a Clean Environment (VCE) is an example of the adaptive strategy applied to an issue already subject to formal government proceedings. This group, members of the Virginia Beer Wholesalers and Soft Drink Associations, created a climate of opinion receptive to alternative solutions to roadside litter. The efforts of VCE resulted in the death, in legislative committee, of a restrictive "bottle bill" and the substitution of the Model Litter Control

---

[2]Ian Wilson, "Business and the Future: Social Challenge, Corporate Response," in *The Next 25 Years: Crisis and Opportunity*, ed. Andrew A. Spekke (Washington, DC: World Future Society, 1975), p. 150.

Act. This nonpunitive alternative attacks the litter problem without disruptive side effects on business, the consumer, or the development of solid waste management technology.

The National Coal Policy Project is an example of constructive dialogue and accommodation outside the framework of government intervention. It was an effort by two previously warring factions of society to see each other's point of view on the use of the nation's coal reserves. The Project was started in 1976 when Gerald L. Decker, corporate energy manager for Dow Chemical, approached Larry Moss, former president of the Sierra Club, to suggest a working compromise between knowledgeable and respected industrialists and environmentalists.

The policy project leaders adopted guidelines recommended by Milton R. Wessel in *The Rule of Reason*, a sustained essay on how to transform issue differences into mutually acceptable programs. Under the aegis of Georgetown University's Center for Strategic and International Studies, longtime adversaries agreed on more than 200 steps that the nation can take to use its coal reserves to the optimum advantage of both public and private interests.

Dynamic

The third mode of response is the **Dynamic,** or pro-active. This strategy anticipates and attempts to shape the direction of public policy decisions by determining the theater of war, the weapons to be used, and the timing of the battle itself. In other words, the company employing the dynamic strategy directs change by developing *real* solutions to *real* problems with *real* results. The work of the beverage and container industries, this time in California, illustrates this option. In 1977, California had no statewide restrictive container law, or "bottle bill." Rather than opposing such a bill, or compromising to address the aesthetic problem of roadside litter, industry became the leading advocate of S.B. 650. This law combines many of the social/behavioral approaches to solving the litter problem through education, increased availability of equipment, and enforcement of anti-litter laws. Significantly, S.B. 650 also incorporates several real low and high technology solutions; e.g., recycling and solid waste management, to the problem of resource recovery, re-use, and the creation of energy from solid waste. This approach not only addresses the visual problem of litter, but also offers solutions to the very real problems described. In short, industry selected a dynamic strategy and became proponents of positive social change. At the same time, industry protected its current production and distribution patterns as determined by competition and consumer choice.

The Dynamic option can be used in combination with the Reactive and Adaptive to create a fourth change strategy option that is pragmatically realistic over time. This combination can work to address short-, mid-, and long-range problems by priority.

Timing is vital in making such strategic choices and changes. The manager's timing decisions are significantly influenced by five forces: (1) the risks inherent in the situation; (2) the manager's confidence in his or her information; (3) the accuracy of the manager's forecasts; (4) the likelihood that the matter may be self-healing; and (5) the direction of affairs.[3] Timing is also essential for the development of editorial and political support for the company's position.

---

[3]Richard H. Buskirk, *Handbook of Managerial Tactics* (Boston, MA: Cahners Books, Inc., 1976), p. 136.

RE-ACTIVE VS. DYNAMIC

As suggested earlier, the "bottle bill" exemplifies the corporate response choices represented by the three response modes indicated in the Model.

When state after state, led by Oregon, began to "solve" the litter problem by restrictive legislation, usually in the form of can and bottle taxation, container manufacturers had three options.

The first was to be *re-active*, to pour resources into fighting such legislation on a state by state basis. This worked in some states, but failed to halt the trend. The president of a major beverage association used the old expression, "Let's stonewall this issue," in referring to states such as Mississippi where the beverage industry had confidence in its "control" of legislatures.

As the re-active approach demonstrated increasing weaknesses (and political defeats), some container manufacturers moved to the *adaptive* response. In effect, this represented an attempt to compromise, to meet partially the objectives of the increasingly strong environmental groups out to "ban the can."

A few companies, notably Reynolds Metals with its aluminum can recycling programs, and American Can with its attempt to transfer public attention to the total solid waste problem, moved from the "Let's stonewall this one" posture into the dynamic response mode. This can be characterized as "Let's change the theater of war." American Can dramatically illustrated this shift by pouring millions of capital into a waste-to-energy, waste recovery program and by literally buying Milwaukee's 300,000 tons of garbage per year, recycling it, almost eliminating landfills, and providing a large fraction of greater Milwaukee's energy need by pelletizing garbage as a fuel substitute for oil.

The fact that corporate restructuring at American Can has eliminated its strategic solution to the entire problem of solid waste disposal does not minimize the goal it set: *dynamic* action on a major issue, at a profit.

CHAPTER EIGHT

Issue Action Programming

"The great end of life is not
knowledge, but action."

—*Thomas Henry Huxley*
Technical Education *(1879)*

Policy to Support the Selected Change Strategy

After the choice of a method or plan for responding to each issue, senior management must adopt **Policy to Support the Selected Change Strategy,** and thereafter give total executive commitment to it. Policy sets the broad limits within which the *Issue Action Program* takes place. Within these limits, public policy managers become strategists, responsible for organizing and coordinating tactical resources to reach the issue action program goal.

At the center of the Issue Action Program step is the familiar core of the public policy process. In this step, the corporation brings together prior research, analysis, and priority setting to become an effective participant in the public policy debate.

Objectives and Goal

In deciding the outcome desired from the action program, the organization establishes a **Goal,** the first ring in this step. A goal provides program direction and thrust in terms that are broad, yet specific as possible. In the next ring, **Objectives** are determined. These program objectives are narrower in focus and expressed in definite, measurable terms. Together, the goal and objectives set the standards for reviewing and evaluating the performance of issue managers.

Strategies

In the **Strategies** ring, the issue manager identifies the **organizational, political, psychological,** and **economic** means and resources he or she will marshall to provide maximum support for reaching the program's goal and objectives. An interdisciplinary outlook, drawing elements from organizational development, political science, social science, and economics, is essential to facilitate the manager's selection of strategies.

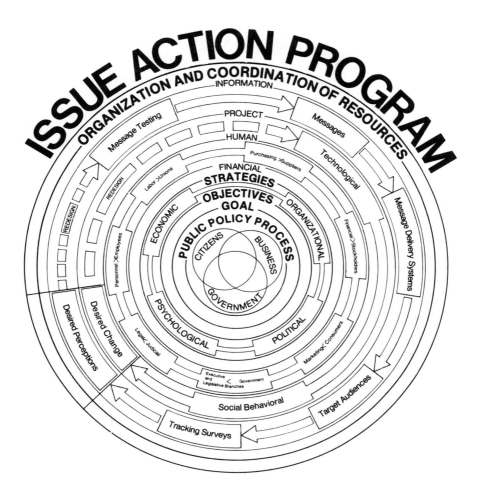

PERFORMANCE EVALUATING TOOL

As often happens, the availability of the Issue Management Process Model reveals an unanticipated dividend. Whereas profit center managers can stand or fall on their profit contribution when the annual Performance and Evaluations Review rolls around, there has been no objective way of evaluating (in terms of compensation) the performance of men and women in the issue/policy areas.

The Model changes this. The evaluators have available all the factors in all four stages of the Model as they appear in the concentric circles. The "complete" issue manager must have training and skills in every stage of the process. It will no longer be enough to be a specialist in any single stage—at least not enough for the aspirant to high corporate officership in issue/policy management.

The performance and evaluation group can thus create bar charts, measuring strengths or weaknesses in each of the disciplines listed in the model.

Professional issue management demands linear progression from Issue Identification through Issue Action Programming. However, the compensation and performance evaluators can reverse the patterns in studying the employee's competence at each of the stages.

Organization and Coordination of Resources

Once the strategies are chosen, **Organization and Coordination of Resources** are vital to program efficiency and effectiveness. These resources, divided in the four subrings, are Financial, Human, Project, and Information. They represent the tactical resources for developing the issue action program and achieving its specific goal. Tactics are simply planned maneuverings of money, people, deeds, and information to execute a program. Indeed, an issue action program itself may be a mere tactic in a larger program for the achievement of a broader corporate goal.

The innermost of the four tactical rings, **Financial,** is self-explanatory. How much money is the organization willing to spend to manage a given issue? Allocation of money is not enough; economic assets alone will not make problems go away. The realistic issue manager, like a plant manager facing a production decision, must carefully allocate financial, intellectual, and time resources to maximize acquisition and application of the available human, project, and information resources.

Financial Resources

TRADE ASSOCIATION STAKE

Many companies tend to delegate their issue/policy considerations to their industry associations. "We're too small to do this ourselves," is the standard comment. "Besides we pay dues to our association to worry about those things."

A sad fact, however, is that most association managements know precisely what they're supposed to be *against* (the reactive mode), but only in most general terms what they are *for* (the dynamic mode). Issues can be "stonewalled" for only so long; then emerging trends overcome the Maginot Line complex.

For example, as stated earlier, on March 23, 1983, the Board of Directors of the American Society of Association Executives adopted issue priority positions on 15 issues (reported in *CPI,* April 15, 1983). Without a single exception, each issue was emerging, and the ASAE Board vowed to fight all of them.

There are notable exceptions—but few—to the industry association resistance to accept either the *adaptive* or *dynamic* postures. Exceptions certainly include the Aluminum Association of America, where the Darden Chambliss foresight has paid dividends. Another exception is the Chemical Manufacturer's Association, where issue management at its best has Jon Holtzman as its champion. The National Association of Manufacturers has begun to provide issue briefs to its members.

For the most part, however, association managers find it safer—and more productive in membership fees—to *attack* "disruptive trends," rather than try to *participate* through issue management, in actually forming the policies that will affect their members.

CPI (January 15, 1983) has advised companies to resign from associations which make no effort to learn issue/policy disciplines.

Human Resources

The next set of resources is labelled **Human.** These resources include familiar line and staff functions and their accessible constituencies: **Financial/Stockholders, Marketing/Consumers, Government Relations/Executive and Legislative Officials, Legal/Judiciary, Personnel/Employees, Labor Relations/Unions.** Others could be added: Press Relations/Media, Sales/Wholesalers, etc. The astute executive will realize that the functional managers listed here are a daily source of feedback, as well as an information channel to earn constituency understanding and support for the members drawn from both line and staff. On the basis of this experience, William H. Gruber and John S. Niles say that the new management of future firms "will effectively integrate the experience and intuition of line executives with the specialized knowledge of staff professionals."[1]

Line and staff roles can and must be blended, without disrupting the existing organizational structure, to integrate management resources to improve corporate advocacy in the public policy debate. The Sun Company, for example, has started this process in two ways. First, some Sun executives have recognized the need to apply a systems approach to issue management decision-making and to long-range public policy planning. Second, they have created discrete, yet interrelated functional networks within the existing organizational structure that can be adapted to public policy management.

Project Resources

Before the human resources can effectively sustain the company's position on the issue, they must have credible **projects,** the next ring outward, to build a platform for their communications. Advertising, speeches, or newspaper stories are important and valuable in influencing attitudes and opinions. But as Irving S. Shapiro, now retired chairman of the Business Roundtable and former chief executive officer of DuPont, says: "You build confidence not by taking ads in newspapers but by performance that convinces the public that what you're doing is compatible with its interests."[2]

Whether the issue action program persuades its audiences is not as dependent, then, upon the messages used as upon the quality of the projects or deeds the messages represent. Effective projects are those *deeds* which not only build a case for the organization's position, but also represent

[1]William H. Gruber and John S. Niles, *The New Management* (New York: McGraw-Hill Book Co., 1976), p. x.
[2]"Today's Executive: Private Steward and Public Servant," *Harvard Business Review*, Vol. 56, No. 2 (1978), p. 97.

the development of real solutions to real problems by priority. There are two types of projects—**technological** and **social/behavioral.**

An example of the technological project is Reynolds Metals' successful establishment of aluminum can recycling centers. Originally, these centers were part of a public relations program to provide the company with a visible answer to its litter-minded critics; since that time resource recovery at Reynolds has become a self-sustaining profit center.

The National Bank of Detroit's (NBD) Criminal Justice Forum is an illustrative social/behavioral project. NBD felt that the city's soaring crime rate and the resulting social unrest was a threat to society and its own business. NBD sponsored a series of public forums at which nearly 20,000 citizens heard the facts, discussed them, and then responded with letters and votes to change those parts of the criminal justice system which were failing in practice. The citizen action generated by the forums has resulted in several new state laws on crime which are acceptable to the bank and to the public. Technological and social/behavioral projects can also be combined, as previously illustrated by the industry-sponsored bill, S.B. 650, in California.

If successful in solving or redefining the problem in the minds of concerned audiences, the selected projects will bring about the **desired change.** If the projects are not successful, the manager must **redesign,** delete, combine, expand or intensify them to build a more credible platform for the information program.

Information Resources

The next and last tactical resource ring is **Information.** As illustrated, it begins with **message testing,** and then proceeds on the basis of what Harold D. Lasswell says is "a convenient way to describe an act of communication: Who, Says

What, in Which Channel, to Whom, with What Effect."[3] Human resources mobilized as credible organization and third party spokespersons are the "who" of the communications process. Projects build platforms to support a hierarchy of **messages,** subject to message testing. Once the messages have been tested and approved, there are only three message tactics: what to communicate, when to communicate, and when not to communicate.

The ideal communication program does not rely solely on mass media, but rather blends mass media with interpersonal **message delivery systems.** The blending should be based on such considerations as the power of each delivery system to inform, persuade, and invoke desired action. Although the mass media are the source of most information received by the public, this does not mean that public opinion can be easily formed, or swayed, by such means. Communications researchers have found that information which does not support an individual's beliefs creates psychological tension (cognitive dissonance). The individual is generally less receptive to information that does not agree with his or her predispositions (selective exposure); human beings will single out those media and messages which support their biases (selective perception). When a person recalls information which enhances his or her needs, values, and views (and suppresses opposing facts and arguments), it is termed selective retention.

In other words, the mass media are probably most effective in two situations. First, mass media

[3]Harold D. Lasswell, "The Structure and Function of Communication in Society," in *The Process and Effects of Mass Communications,* ed. Wilbur Schramm and Donald F. Roberts (Urbana, IL: University of Illinois Press, 1972), p. 84.

should be used when they appear to have a good chance of influencing those already disposed to the corporate position on an issue, and only then. Second, activist and public interest groups have demonstrated that the mass media can be used to create the impression of a large and stable political support base, which may or may not reflect reality. Emotions often surround complex public policy issues, and the press generally treats the issues superficially, because of its limited time, space, and staff. Thus, the managers of the action program should seek mass media coverage in situations where they can select the presentation and message format to reach target audiences.

Target audiences should be placed on a continuum of attitudes and opinions, ranging from the hardcore adversaries with a negative attitude toward the corporate position on the issue to those already friendly and predisposed. The distinction this continuum makes between attitudes and opinions of various target audiences is important. Transient opinions often become ingredients in the constant, gradual reformation of attitudes. In other words, *an opinion is a belief stronger than an impression, but weaker than an attitude which indicates a readiness to act.*

In the middle of this continuum are the groups and individuals whose opinions are probably changeable, pro or con, within a short time frame. As any good politician knows, elections are won by strengthening the support of current constituents, while communicating with the swing voters (undecided) to neutralize the claims of adversaries. But to be persuasive, the substance of selected communications must be compatible with the dynamic social, economic, and political forces in the environment where the swing voters live and work.

Communications theory and research will help the issue manager design an acceptable information program, reaching target audiences through appropriate media with credible sources and messages. **Tracking surveys** will measure the effects of communications on groups and individuals, at varying times during the program. This research will determine whether the campaign is creating the **desired perceptions** necessary to earn public support for corporate policy. If desired perceptions are not created, the Model provides for the **redesign** of communication programming.

To earn **Support for the Policy Decision,** an accepted management technique, such as critical path analysis, should be used to schedule, coordinate, and control the many discrete, yet interdependent tactical resources. Application of such techniques will enhance effective **"Accomplishment of the Issue Action Program Goal,"** which in turn leads to the last step, Evaluation of Results.

Support for the Policy Decision

NEW DIMENSIONS

The reader will note that the communications process is the outer ring—the penultimate stage—of the entire integrated issue management process. This is a source of dismay to many professional communicators. Many seem to think its placement in the issue management process rules them out of the action, and endangers their hard-won roles in the corporate structure.

The exact opposite is true. The will and effort on the part of public relations/public affairs managers to comprehend and master *all* issue management disciplines will open the door to managerial dimensions they have never yet enjoyed. It remains to be seen how many of them will "seize this nettle."

Evaluation of Results

Although the organization may have accomplished its issue action program goal, it has not yet completed the issue management process. Executives must evaluate the *real* versus *intended* program results and subject the program managers to performance review. They must also continue monitoring anticipated social, economic, and political changes. The Issue Management Process Model provides this framework, combining a management philosophy with an ongoing systems process to help executives identify, analyze, and manage public policy issues in a populist society experiencing discontinuous change.

Conclusion

"These are the times," says John De Butts, former chairman and chief executive officer of A.T.&T., "that demand not a dramatic leadership but a reasoning one, a leadership disciplined by experience in matching aims to the resources necessary to achieve them, a leadership unafraid of complexity and confident that complexity can be managed."[4]

From complete adaptation and use of the Issue Management Process Model, three conclusions clearly emerge:

(1) Most, if not all, of the contemporary corporate or institutional practices variously labelled public relations, public affairs, government relations, and communications (which in combination represent annual expenditures of billions of dollars) *are inadequate in themselves for systems management of public policy issues.* They are, rather, aggregations of specific skills and techniques for use when, as, and if the management of issues requires them.

---

[4]John D. De Butts, "The Management of Complexity," in *Management for the Future,* ed. Lewis Benton (New York: McGraw-Hill Book Co., 1978), p. 86.

NO STATUS QUO

Refer to the entire Model for a critically important realization. During the precise timespan
in which a company or institution may have
been managing its highest priority issue, the
economic, political and social milieu in which
it had been operating is subject to continuous
change.

Every identified issue demands continuous
monitoring and measurement. Fighting yesterday's battles has unrewarding aspects.

---

(2) Just as the older functions of personnel,
employee relations, and labor relations are
being rapidly regrouped into the larger executive concept of human resources, *it is inevitable that corporations will create a new
senior or executive vice president for public
policy.* (See Chapter 14.)

(3) *The public policy manager will use a systems planning methodology.* It will integrate public policy considerations into
decentralized operations, subject to appropriate corporate controls. In other words, this
methodology will be a "who-does-what-and-
when" roadmap for injecting the issue management process, described herein, into the
corporation's overall planning system and
into each of its operating units.

Finally, this systems approach to public policy
management is precisely applicable to the decision-making process on *every* major issue that
confronts the profit-center executive.

Issue Management: Growth, Obstacles, Present Status

CHAPTER NINE

Carrying The Message To Garcia

"If we could first know where we are (issue identification) and whither we are tending (issue analysis), we could better judge what to do (issue priority setting) and how to do it (issue action programming)."

—Abraham Lincoln on Issue Management

Believing that there are reservoirs of talent within the external relations field that want very badly to assume more managerial responsibilities, I jumped at the opportunity to keynote the annual conference of the Canadian Public Relations Society, in 1980, on the subject, "A Whole New World of Public Policy."

This speech, adapted here from its appearance in *Vital Speeches* (August 15, 1980), signified an effort to transform the theory of issue management into a pragmatic roadmap by which it can be transferred to corporate and institutional management reality. Whether it deserves inclusion as evolving "literature" may be questionable. It serves some aspirants well, and is ignored by others. In any event, here it is, in large part:

"A Whole New World of Public Policy"

It is quite true that my transition from student and practitioner of sound communications practice into an exponent of our profession's inevitably larger role in the senior management structure makes me an embarrassment to our more traditionally-minded colleagues.

Why doesn't Chase leave well enough alone? Here we are, 1,400 in CPRS, 11,000 in PRSA, 600 in International Public Relations Association, with at least ten times as many others around the world engaging in the useful art of communications. Why rock the boat? Look at the progress we have made in less than 75 years. Why not just extol our past, and congratulate each other on how many of us are becoming vice presidents?

In partial answer, a cartoon several years ago in the *New Yorker* magazine portrayed an aging and sagging woman standing nude on a shallow beach, saying defiantly: "Public opinion no longer bothers me." This cartoon perfectly illustrates and explains my indifference to—and compassion for—sources of the occasional barbed comment that issue managers are rocking the boat. Why must they insist that the new and larger opportunities ahead demand all the old arts *plus* the new management sciences that are available? But more of this later.

My own first line to classes of candidates for the Master's degree in Business Administration is at least as pointed: "Nothing that management did yesterday is good enough for tomorrow." It represents a profound conviction that the intelligent, attractive people at staff or consulting levels in external affairs are being called by historical development to be the movers and shakers in senior management itself.

If the next few remarks sound like the ghost that stalks at Banquo's feast—and they may have that effect—they are only intended as benchmarks of problems the communicator faces today. Here are only a few at random.

"The Ghost That Stalks at Banquo's Feast"

Example No. 1: Anthony di Lorenzo, after years as chief public relations officer at General Motors, has said that companies see their public relations directors as "glad-handers, courtiers, and mouthpieces." The senior officers, he said, "have low expectations" of their public relations staff, "especially with regard to their ability to handle crises."

Example No. 2: A recent president of the Public Relations Society of America, Pat Jackson, asked for a protest to the American Management Associations on the decision to include its text on public relations in a book on marketing, and its other decision to abandon reference to public relations as a profession.

Example No. 3: Within the past year, at least ten very large American companies have replaced their distinguished public relations leaders with officers derived from either profit center management or from the legal profession. In not one single instance does the new officership carry the title of public relations, an ominous portent for the traditionalists.

It is said that he who runs may read. The Old Testament's handwriting on the wall, "mene mene tekel, upharsin," roughly translated, means being weighed in the balance and found wanting. This is the fate of those who resist change.

But there is a larger framework for concern about both the present and future of the external relations functions. In 1950, by rough estimate the Fortune 500 companies in the States spent about $300 million on the still young profession calling itself public relations, not including cost of institutional advertising. By 1979, again roughly, they spent perhaps $3 billion, a ten-fold increase. For all intents and purposes, corporate relations activities could be said to have flourished over this 29-year period.

But let's take another look at the two years, 1950 and 1979. In 1950, by all available polls, about 85 percent of the American public registered general approval and endorsement of private sector management. (Hang on to your hats!) By the same polls, in 1979 that approval had turned to suspicion and distrust, and only 15 percent registered confidence in management of large institutions.

By crude mathematics, this is a drop in public approval of about 70 points, *and* it occurred during the same time span that companies were increasing their investment in public relations, by a factor of 1,000 percent, to achieve a desired milieu of public harmony.

There was a play a few years ago entitled "A Funny Thing Happened on the Way to the Forum." From a senior management point of view, it was inevitable that the CEOs would begin to notice that their dramatic investment in improved communications had not been very effective, at least as a source of public understanding and support.

Example No. 4: In 1976, I conducted a mail poll of the chief executive officers of the Fortune 500 companies, with more than 200 responses, and re-ran the same poll in 1979 with comparable returns. Let us deal with responses to only two questions.

First, the questionnaire asked what percentage of their working hours these CEOs were spending on "external relations"—that is, public policy problems over and above their concerns for profit center management.

In 1976, the average percentage of executive time spent on "external relations" was about 20 percent. This poll was consistent with a canvass of about 1,500 senior executives attending a Conference Board session. In responding to almost the same basic question, the majority, by a show of hands, said they were now devoting more than half their working hours to public issues and public policy. *Business Week* noted this with surprise.

The final question in the survey was even more significant: It asked whether the CEO had as much confidence in his external relations management team as he had in his profit center colleagues. In 1976, only 20 percent expressed dissatisfaction with the company's public relations/public affairs management team. In 1979, this had risen to an astounding 60 percent!

Small wonder that despite all technical advances being made by external relations practitioners, more and more companies are turning to talent outside these ranks for their highest public policy officerships!

These lugubrious examples only sample the smorgasbord of serious problems that traditional external relationists face as a profession. A distinguished Canadian, in a recent letter, summarized much of this situation: "For years," he wrote, "I have heard of the terrible struggle public relations people have had to gain the ear of top management. Now, it seems we may not have terribly much to say into that ear."

One can fully understand, but still respectfully disagree. There is an early American midwestern axiom that the wise date "goes home from the dance with the guy (or girl) that brung her." One of my own daughters, at the advanced age of six, came home from school quite puzzled about the U.S. pledge of allegiance to the flag and to the Republic. The way she had heard it was, "I public relations to the flag of the United States of America and to the Republicans for which it stands."

I pledge more allegiance than ever to the allied crafts of public relations, public affairs, and communications. Potentially, we have more to say into the senior executive ear than any other comparable group of intelligent disciplined men and women. But we face the pungent question asked by William White in his book, *Is Anybody Listening?* Are we thinking, talking, and writing in yesterday's out-dated language as we move into the increasingly politicized world of tomorrow?

Alfred North Whitehead, in *Aims of Education,* suggested that adolescent minds should be filled with basic information, facts, and techniques in order that they can be available as tools when the child-turned-adult faces the problems of maturity. But this inference was also clear: For a person or a profession to maintain an obsession with tools and techniques, at the expense of the broad considerations of mankind, is to guarantee a permanent and unattractive adolescence.

Let's be clear. Without skills, tools, and techniques, we are like doctors with no knowledge of anatomy or chemistry. We are poseurs, or, in blunter language, phonies. But even the most advanced techniques, sold as ammunition for a "hired gun" to the highest bidder, without regard to the social consequences of their use, constitutes precisely the crime with which public relations is most frequently charged. In Tony di Lorenzo's harsh appraisal, its practitioners are "glad-handers, courtiers, and mouthpieces." The profession neither deserves such a put-down nor enjoys it. However, these labels do represent a widespread image. Unless individuals now bearing the label of public relations and its allied crafts destroy this image by their own upward striving and broader horizons, that image will effectively prevent them from having *any* substantial role in the new world.

The Gospel of St. Luke remarks of Christ that "He grew in wisdom, stature, and in favor with God and man."

In more modern terms, how do external affairs staff advisors cease being that horrible but frequently used epithet: "the chairman's boys or girls," and achieve in their own right, "wisdom, stature, and favor with God and man?"

The answer is that, in a systems world, the traditionalists must add the hard disciplines of the evolving social sciences into training and practice. They must demonstrate by discipline and process that their skills and techniques are applicable to solution of the social, economic, and political problems that have impact on executive decision-making.

Let us, as Father Divine used to say, "tangibilitate the subject." In both the classroom and in corporate seminars, I ask line and staff managers to role-play the chief executive officer, and to brainstorm the major issues of our time that, in each individual's case, represent problems vitally affecting the future of his or her organization.

The Issue Management Seminar

The shouted-out list of issues, written on black-boards, has never numbered less than 80, with 125 as the top. The technique, after about 30 minutes of this exercise, is to express all-out admiration for what the participants have done, and to say that such a process deserves a name. For lack of a better term, we call it the issue identification process.

Then I suggest that a number of the issues listed seem to fall into broader categories. Air, water, and land pollution, for instance, along with solid waste disposal, would seem to fall into a broad category of environmental issues. Will the group now say what other general categories they perceive into which most or all of the scores of single issues would fall? Usually in less than 20 minutes, the role-playing CEOs have produced anywhere from 15 to 25 categories. Once again I compliment them, suggesting that they have now filtered a hundred or so issues through their own experience and judgment facilities. If they don't have a better name for it, perhaps they can agree that they have just demonstrated the issue analysis process.

What happens next? How many major issue categories do they think their companies can handle at any given time? Each "CEO" is then asked to list in writing the 10 categories of major issues which he or she believes to be of greatest importance to the company and to the role-playing officer. This usually takes about 15 minutes. At that point each CEO is asked to number the order of priorities from 1 to 10, sign the list, and hand it in.

Please observe that at no single point has the teacher interjected or superimposed personal views on the group. They themselves are creating a process approach to the management of public issues. When their list of priorities has been established, I compliment them again, and observe that since everything has to be called something, they have just created their own set of issue change strategy options, or, in simpler terms, the issue priority setting process.

Finally, I suggest that it makes no sense to exert all this thoughtful effort in identifying, analyzing, and setting priorities on public issues which have major effects on their companies, and on themselves, without organizing to do something about them. How can these dedicated issue managers achieve total executive commitment unless they create issue action programming, and achieve tangible and bottom-line results?

This leads to creation of task forces, usually one for each of the four or five issues to which they—not the instructor—have assigned high priority. Each task force is asked to elect its own chairman, preferably a profit center manager, and to create an issue action program appropriate both to the issue and to the company.

After a working interval of not less than two hours, or perhaps overnight, each task force reassembles before its fellow seminarians—who are now role-playing members of the Board of Directors. Their issue action programs are presented, discussed, voted up, down, or possibly sent back for further consideration. If a task force has a member who wishes to present a minority report, the "Board" hears it, affirming or rejecting it as the case may be.

When all the issue action programs have been considered, approved, disapproved, or returned for further study, then and only then do we unveil the Issue Management Process Model, using slides. But something of great importance has happened: *The Model presents itself not as the product of an outside "expert," but as a photograph of what the role-playing CEOs have themselves created.* Thus avoided are the sad consequences of the NIH, or Not-Invented-Here syndrome. No one "who doesn't know the unique conditions of our company" has tried to superimpose any alien ideas.

Describing this exercise has a double purpose. The first is to recommend this or similar type seminars for any corporation or institution. The second is more germane to the title discussed here, "A Whole New World of Public Policy."

Note that at no point did a professional communicator present a superimposed program designed to create better understanding. Instead, what happened was a *joint* effort of line *and* staff managers to do four things: (1) to identify the important issues that affect executive decision-making; (2) to analyze and classify them into broad categories—or issue analysis; (3) to set priorities, taking into account the non-controllability, semi-controllability, or controllability of the issues; and (4) to devise a company-wide issue action program to achieve real-world results. (Note the applicability of Abraham Lincoln's comment at the beginning of this chapter.)

While every technique known to communication arts is implicit in the process, those who follow this technique simply end-run the current "image" disadvantages described in the earliest part of this discourse. They no longer resemble Tony di Lorenzo's dismal description of relations practitioners as "glad-handers, courtiers, and mouthpieces."

But what has the participant *become?* He or she has become the exponent of soundly-conceived action programs by which a company or institution can become a participant in the public-policy decision-making process. The CEO role-players will have graduated from the myth that they are merely interpreters or communicators of existing policy. They will have demonstrated a capacity to move into the frontier of new management science, and will have earned executive consideration—and reward—that comes from the new perception of true abilities—the *capacity to contribute to corporate strategic planning.*

Further, the newly-established issue manager will have demonstrated—frequently to the astonishment of the senior executive—that there is a disciplined systems process that the CEO has reason to respect, in the same fashion that he or she respects systems management of production, finance, marketing, and other major profit-center operations.

Is this merely theory, or does pragmatic evidence support it as fact? *Dun's Business Month* (June, 1980) notes that corporate planning is growing and gaining internal clout during this recession. Kevin Phillips, in his *Business and Public Affairs Fortnightly* (June 15, 1980) states that recruiters report that demand for strategic planners far outstrips their availability. Wearing my own executive search hat, I have looked for a woman to join the strategic planning staff of a major company at $60,000 per year. One corporation, in 1981, sought help to find a Public Policy Issue Director at $80,000. (In 1983, he receives about $100,000.) The client assumes that all the communications skills are implicit in issue management and strategic planning capabilities.

Pragmatic Evidence

Robert Felton, of McKinsey & Company, stresses that strategic planning involves weighing and building flexibility around a number of external factors, especially competition and government/regulatory impact. This is the issue manager's daily bread. Finally, he says, the strategic planning function must become part of the daily routine at all levels of the organization.

Again, the role-player will have perceived that every reference just quoted is totally consistent with the purposes of the issue management process, and one's own evolution from staff to executive management. The nettle is there to seize.

The Wall Street Journal (June 16, 1980) quoted William Turner, a former U.S. ambassador to the Organization for Economic Cooperation and Development, as follows:

"More and more, non-market factors—economic, political and social (again, the issue manager's daily concerns)—are looking for new tools and mechanisms to monitor these forces effectively and develop early warning systems to anticipate policy changes."

Turner doesn't say, but does imply, that top managers have an allergy against the traditional techniques of attempting to gain public approval by communications alone.

About 200 of the largest companies in America have, within the past seven years, created Board-level committees on issue management, external relations, corporate responsibility, public policy, or similar names to find these "new tools and mechanisms" to monitor the economic, political and social changes which determine either continued corporate stability, or even survival itself.

The Fledgling Leaves the Nest

The professional future of old-line external relations practitioners is divided. A great many will remain competent technicians in communications practice—a role necessary and useful. But the Holy Grail of the profession—a goal which a few leaders have already reached—is evolution to executive or senior vice presidencies-public policy. The new officership, already effectively achieved in a few companies, will be charged with relating and coordinating corporate strategic planning, public relations, public affairs, communications, and government relations into the issue and public policy management function, on an executive level comparable to the line management of production, marketing, and finance.

In short, traditional public relations, understimulated by infantile literature, has been too long in the kindergarten of professional development. It is time for the fledgling to leave the nest. It is time to move boldly into the almost totally politicized new world as *participants* in the public policy decision-making process, rather than remain the tail end of the whip line being cracked by others.

But these goals demand an open mind, and a willingness to "lay aside childish things" and learn the new disciplines of public policy management. They demand a divine discontent with past status, a wholesome skepticism about much of the traditional management literature, and a recognition that what is presented this week as innovative practice was really old 25 years ago.

Precisely as the introduction of public relations into the corporate scheme of things 50 years ago was a quantum jump for a new profession, there is now the need for, and inevitability of, a new quantum leap by those who choose to lead into the new dimensions of public issue and public policy management.

These must be *substantive*, not *trivial*, changes in outlook. In the sense, stated earlier, that "public opinion no longer bothers me," I have no objection to semantic changes, *if* they serve a purpose. As early as December 15, 1978, *Corporate Public Issues and Their Management (CPI)* launched a trial balloon about a change in the name of Public Relations Society of America to Public Policy Society of America. About a hundred letters and calls praised the idea. Quite a number were also appalled. Three years later, PRSA did create a national Public Affairs Section, a step in this direction.

Unless existing organizations assume this new public policy mission, others are waiting in the wings to fill the vacuum created by non-action. The North American Society for Corporate Planning is merely one example. The Issues Management Association is another.

This appraisal of the future has tried to do three things: **(1)** express confidence in the qualities, competence, and capacity of professional communications to accept larger challenges; **(2)** review some of the hazards they face right now; and **(3)** demonstrate that:

Whatever the labels, enormous opportunities beckon the external relationists; and also, they must become the disciplined exponents of sound public issue and public policy management, because that's where the action is. . . .

To conclude: No management (or management technique) good enough for yesterday is good enough for tomorrow. Destiny will inevitably take surprising twists and turns. Only one thing is sure: conventional public relations will decrease in influence and prestige. But the open-minded professional will find satisfaction and reward in dedicating present and potential talents to the brave new world of issue/public policy management.

"Managing Public Policy Issues," and the speech just presented, along with *CPI* 24 times a year, serve as a kind of fever chart of the trials, tribulations, and accomplishments of the issue management process. Applied pragmatically, they represent the birth pangs of what is now a rapidly growing literature. Case histories of issue management in action, ably conceived, implemented, and presented, have added substance at scores of corporate and professional group forums.

Unfortunately, apart from *CPI*, which chooses to summarize only the essence of these case histories, there is no journal to record them in detail. Inevitably, there will be such a journal, either originated and sustained by a professional society, or by entrepreneurs in the publishing field.

In the meantime, the body of literature—without which there can be no profession—grows apace.

CHAPTER TEN

Obstacles to Issue Management

"It is the business of the future
to be dangerous."

—*Alfred North Whitehead*

**Six
Obstacles
Stand Out:**

1. Ignorance of managers themselves of evolving literature—and inexperience in management of policy;
2. Fear of and resistance to innovation, at both senior and middle management levels;
3. The tendency among professional societies and organizations to institutionalize, homogenize, or degrade their original objectives;
4. The Ph.D. professorial and frequent management "club" antagonism to any idea "not invented here;"
5. The too-frequent proclivity of chief executive officers to delegate responsibility for external relations/issue-policy management/public policy considerations to upper middle-management without regard to their past experience. This leads to resultant hiring practices based on conventional job descriptions that aren't adequate to yesterday's—much less tomorrow's—needs.
6. The Neanderthal urge to fight fire with fire.

Each of these obstacles is interrelated with all the others.

**Management
Ignorance**

Taking them in order, we must remind ourselves that new professional disciplines do not spring "full-blown from the brow of Jove." By 1977, several years after the concept of issue management was introduced at American Can and a year after it was first publicly named in *CPI*, Barry Jones and other associates had cross-indexed 550 separate books, theses, and corporate case histories, each of which contributed to this logical evolutionary concept: Issue/policy management's time has come, and professional skill in this area is at least as important as skilled profit-center management. Additions to this basic bibliography, case histories, speeches and articles, accumulate almost daily. Just as all the precursor literature contributed to the issue/policy management concept up to about 1978, since that time issue management practices have contributed to the later literature. Hundreds of scholars and authors have ably revealed the "why" of issue management, but have ignored its application.

With issue management's clearly established indebtedness to past and present thought and experience, the reader may understand this author's vexation when a public relations counsellor announced at a public forum that "Chase has stolen his ideas from Igor Ansoff." The same philosopher, during the same speech, stated that "issue management is another way of CYA (covering your ass)."

Certainly all students of issue management do owe a debt to Igor Ansoff and to at least 500 other authors with the courage and wisdom to predict the end of traditional molds.

Resistance to issue management has sometimes inspired oracular indignation. One Board member of PRSA was moved to write to Teresa Yancey Crane, publisher of *CPI*:

> "So-called 'issue management' existed long before Howard Chase formalized it into his own money-making proposition. It has been and continues to be practiced as a normal part of the public relations responsibilities of professional practitioners everywhere.
>
> "Be aware that more than a few of us are tired of Howard's pretensions to being the great creator of a new 'wheel.' The crown doesn't fit!"

Fear of and Resistance to Innovation

The second of the listed obstacles is closely akin to the attitude just expressed. After all, as shown in Chapter I, the functions of public relations and later public affairs are themselves in evolution, and even their names are less than 70 years old. Since 1948, dues-paying membership in the three "organizational lodges" representing these functions have expanded by a factor of 60 (Public

Relations Society of America—PRSA, Public Affairs Council—PAC, and International Association of Business Communicators—IABC).

The founders and motivators of this amazing growth faced and overcame their own problems with tradition. Management hostility or apathy towards communications, even though much of it has now disappeared, created a functional psychosis even among some of those innovators. It quite resembles the pioneers' practice each night of forming a circle of their prairie schooners to ward off Indians and wolves. "We have come so far against obstacles," they seem to say. "Don't bother us now."

It is an ancient axiom that both human beings and animals, once having established their "turf," will fight fiercely to defend it. The disciplines of issue management, which in all logic should be an extension or expansion of turf hard-won by public relations/public affairs pioneers, are instead thought by some to be a menace to their own domain.

Tendency to Homogenize Professional Society Objectives

This individualized fear of innovation, even among heirs of leaders who had been innovative themselves in creating the values inherent in the public relations/public affairs techniques, is closely related to the third listed obstacle: the tendency among professional societies and organizations to institutionalize or homogenize original objectives and values.

PRSA, for example, was originated to bring together, professionally, the abilities and aspirations of men and women to improve the human or public relationships between corporate and social entities. Its founders, of whom I was one of six, have never once denigrated the importance of communications techniques. Rather, they are major *tools*. Anyone who cares to read the first four bound volumes of the *Public Relations Journal* will find abundant evidence of a profound vision: Public relations was to be an operating philosophy to create a milieu in which even adversarial groups could find a common harmony.

However, with the passage of years, the tools for some became more important than the vision. The *HOW-TO*—How-To write a press release, How-To conduct special events, How-To work with media, How-To handle financial relations, How-To cope with disasters—all important in themselves—assumed paramount proportions. For many, but by no means all, a Society intended to be professional evolved into an association primarily for the sharing of techniques. The substitution of specific skills for a larger social destiny is by no means confined to the PRSA example. It characterizes a very large share of the 14,000-plus national business associations and hundreds of professional groups in the United States.

Transition from philosophy to techniques had predictable consequences. Instead of remaining what it was intended to be, an "umbrella" organization hospitable to all determined to improve human interrelationships, PRSA, again only as an example, diluted its basic goals by concentration on communications tools. And this led to predictable results. A larger membership, for one thing, but...

The railway public relations specialists withdrew to form their own organization; so did the men and women in educational public relations, financial and investor public relations, the public affairs men and women, and finally the "business communicators" who founded the flourishing IABC—now with 10,000 members.

Another loss was even more poignant. Sensing PRSA's concentration upon individual techniques, a larger number of the senior corporate and social cause managers of public relations either never bothered to join PRSA, or gradually withdrew their memberships.

During all these times—sad by standards suggested here—PRSA assumed more and more the association mantle. Group insurance, concentration on by-laws, politicization and chapter concentration on prestige and influence, the "democratization" process in which numbers of members became more important than quality, all these contributed to a dilution of the original dream. Even Accreditation, a noble cause, has tended to become accreditation in use of techniques, not a sharing of vision and source of public approval. A 1983 PRSA promotion piece for accreditation states that "it (the test) is easier than you think," an approach scarcely designed to increase its importance. The frequent repetitive efforts to mount campaigns of "public relations for public relations" took on the appearance of the Pharisee proclaiming his thanks that he is "not like other men," and generally had the same effect.

Withal, the Society has grown to 11,000 regular members and several thousand student members.

In PRSA, as in many other organizations, techniques are easier to sell than the qualities of leadership. How-to books always sell better than philosophical studies, although the first have short life spans while the second can influence the course of history. This book tries to combine both.

It goes without saying that some of the doctrines described here are not popular with many workers in the vineyard. But there is reason for optimism. PRSA had demonstrated flexibility by creating, in 1982, a special section on Issue Management with excellent leadership. It is a late entry in a burgeoning field, but it demonstrates that the organization is not static. Its Delphi survey on "Strategies for the Eighties," described in *CPI*, August 15, 1983, is a major step towards fundamental self-analysis.

For this author, personally, the professional public relations and public affairs organizations, PRSA and PAC, along with faculty and corporate responsibilities, and editorship of *CPI*, have been ports of entry into the fascinating world of proactive issues and policy management. They have also been the root source of hundreds of cherished friendships.

Of much greater importance, however, is that the membership of these organizations has a running start, through its mastery of communications, into leadership of this fourth revolution of management—*the merging of issues, policy, strategic planning, and risk assessment management into a single entity, governed and administered by a senior officer of public policy.*

The organizations mentioned here have this headstart, if they choose to use it. The results of the 1983 survey of attitudes of PRSA members towards issue management, conducted by Richard N. Bailey, Communication Research Center of the University of Florida, shows that 91 percent of the respondents believe that issue management will play an important part in their own futures.

Antagonism to Ideas

The fourth obstacle, antagonism to ideas, the academic and sometimes managerial lack of interest, neutrality, or downright opposition to the disciplines of issue management, or any new discipline at all, is less easy to understand. Despite the formidable scholarship which preceded and contributed so much to the inevitability of issue/policy management as a senior management function, the fact remains, for stubborn executives, that "it was not invented here."

Harvard's Graduate School of Business Administration, with its case history concentration upon management of profit, has become the security blanket for MBA students everywhere. And justifiably so. Harvard never intended to place intellectual limits, or outer boundaries, on professional management. Yet, paradoxically, that has been the result. There are few business school libraries where the 4,000-plus case histories in profit-management are not the core of their collections. They have had a profound and continuing influence on strategic *profit-planning,* but *they fall very short on management skills and procedures for strategic policy planning and policy management.*

In fact, the Harvard Graduate School of Business Administration's preoccupation with profit has led to its obdurate refusal even to mention public relations, much less the more advanced concept of issue management. This Maginot Line psychosis is hallmark to gradual decline in Harvard's prestige among more contemporary management training institutions. Even Harvard's President Bok has commented on this phenomenon. In any event, academic foot-dragging has been an obstacle to the development of issue management, especially among senior executives who find comfort in hallowed halls.

CEO Delegation of External Relations to Middle Management Traditionalists

The fifth obstacle referred to at the beginning of this chapter is the too-frequent proclivity of chief executive officers to delegate responsibility for external relations/issue-policy management/public policy considerations to upper middle-management, with resultant hiring practices based on yesterday's conventional job descriptions in these areas.

Personal executive searches brought a painful awareness of this proclivity in the early stages of the author's activities at the issue/policy management level. When the corporate budgets coincided with the CEO's decision to hire new talent, and when I was asked to find it, in every case a corporate officer would provide job descriptions of the person the company allegedly wanted. And, in every case, with one exception, these descriptions were outdated catch-alls derived from what the company's personnel or human resources executives *thought* their company wanted. Too many of these departments were merely seeking replacements for traditional external relations practitioners—not a bold advance into public policy participation that society demands. To cautious middle-level hiring managers, the under-achiever is often less of a menace than the over-achiever.

Was maintained traditionalism what the CEO really wanted? To find out, I launched the practice of insisting on a personal interview with the CEO *before* accepting search assignments. The results were eye-opening.

On the very first such occasion, the hiring officer rather resentfully introduced me to the CEO for a "15-minute conference."

After customary pleasantries, I waved a four-page job description before him, with this statement: "This is what your company *says* you want. But I have another question: What do *you* intend to do with this company over the next three years?"

Any desultory nature of the interview vanished into thin air. The 15-minute interview lasted for two hours, and by its end, this searcher knew more about the company's executive aspirations than the officer who had introduced me. Thus, the ultimate candidate for the position was accepted and hired, knowing what the boss really wanted. And when the recommended person was hired, issue/policy management capability had become functional in the company.

This approach, however, remains an exception to the lamentable practice of hiring external relations executives based on yesterday's competencies and not tomorrow's needs. With exactly one other executive placement firm even mentioning issue management as a career, and with none that has ever bothered to explore the implications inherent in the Issue Management Process Model, traditionalists all too often continue to be recommended by these firms, and continue to be hired on the basis of outworn job descriptions. It is not harsh to say that these hiring companies get what they say they wanted, if not what they need.

It is harsh, but true, to conclude that they have asked for too little. They have bought technicians, not participants in public policy formation, not contributors to strategic planning, risk assessment, and executive decision-making.

The Urge to Fight Fire with Fire

The atavistic yen to fight fire with fire, the sixth obstacle, may have its psychic rewards, but is one more major stumbling block to constructive use of issue/policy management principles. General Motors vs. Ralph Nader is a vivid case in point. After Nader had published his book about the Corvair, labelling it *Unsafe at Any Speed,* thereby infuriating GM executives and quite possibly damaging sales (not of the book!), the company chose the Neanderthal type of counter-attack. Having concluded that Nader was reprehensible, dangerous, and quite an unpleasant fellow to have around, it launched its secret investigation into every aspect of his character. Nader promptly sued, and won a judgment of $400,000. Ironically, this sum became the financial basis for the vast expansion of "Nader's Raiders," and brought him more public attention than a dozen books would have achieved.

In issue management terms, General Motors *re*-acted, and lost. Nader had defined his issue, analyzed it, determined that it would have high priority in human and public interest, and then conducted a *pro*-active or dynamic issue action program, and won.

A modern David had once again stunned a Goliath, not with a rock and sling, but with four disciplines of issue management, plus the courage and wit to use them.

Most modern company managements have learned that destruction of the adversary simply isn't possible in an age in which anti-establishment dissidents command at least as much and sometimes more public attention and support than the corporations they attack.

The issue management process, based on the overlapping policy concerns of three separate segments of society—citizens, business, and government—points the way to what today is called "networking." In simplest terms, when an emerging issue threatens to become critical, the issue manager doesn't instinctively "put up his dukes" to fight the invader of establishment policy. Rather, he or she reaches out to leadership of adversarial groups and philosophies to explore rationally with them the possibility that they have interests in common which can be eliminated from the adversarial agenda. (The National Coal Policy Project referred to earlier is a classic example of successful networking. Mary Ann Pires at Texaco, in her work with professional consumer groups, has also demonstrated its value.)

The reader should note that networking has recently taken on a secondary meaning—the process by which the job aspirant sees and talks with as many issue managers as possible, nominally for advice but really in search of employment.

Bruce Smart, chairman and CEO of The Continental Groups, describes the networking term in its original sense, however, and provides a classic text: "It's time to lower our voices, to choke back

The Role of Networking

the accusatory 'bon mot,' and the political cheap shot, in order to resist the urge to 'have a last go at the bastards" (from Smart's speech of November 7, 1982, "Business Beyond Profit," before the Woodlands Conference on Sustainable Societies).

With this conviction stirring at chief executive levels, it is not surprising that Continental is one of the growing list of companies with a Committee on Public Policy, at Board of Directors level.

Summary

The six obstacles to integration of the issue management process into general management listed here are basic, but by no means all-inclusive. There is, for instance, the frequent disposition of the corporate external affairs managers to adapt only the *semantics* of issue management to what they have always done, and somehow managing altogether to ignore the stern *disciplines* presented here in Chapter II. This is the "pouring new wine into old bottles" syndrome. Unfortunately for those who choose these shortcuts, they eventually reveal their own weaknesses and incapacity to reach more elevated management posts. They usually wind up being end-run by their own bosses who see far more clearly than the external relationist how closely management of issues/policy is linked to management of profit.

CHAPTER ELEVEN

Present Status of Issue Management

"Human status ought not to depend
upon the changing demands of the
economic process."

—*William Temple*
The Malverne Manifesto

Issue Management Education

Without even a name until April 15, 1976, the issue management process has grown like Topsy. For six years I had the pioneering opportunity to teach "Public Issues Management" and its disciplines to graduate students in the accredited MBA program at the University of Connecticut, the first such course anywhere. As indicated earlier, the Public Affairs Council holds usually two member seminars each year on "basic" and "advanced" issue management. The Public Relations Society of America, as stated, has created a separate section on the subject. George Washington University, since 1979, has been conducting two seminars each year, with this writer as chairman or interlocutor and program arranger and with 20 to 25 corporate managers as registrants.

Interestingly, these GWU seminars have not been sponsored by either the business school or the public policy departments. On the contrary, they have occurred under the auspices of the Department of Engineering, and the three most recent sessions have concentrated on computerizing the Issue Management Process Model.

About twenty major corporations have authorized "in-house" seminars on issue management for both line and staff executives.

Board-level Committees

An increasing number of corporate Boards now have formalized Issues Committees, a movement spearheaded by General Electric, Sears, and others. Dow has recently changed the title of its Board-level Committee on Social Responsibility to the Issue Management Committee.

Allstate Insurance Companies and Stauffer Chemical Company were the first two corporations to install formalized directorates of issue management. Allied Corporation calls its specialist, Jack Rushing, Director-Public Policy Issues.

Several major publications contained features on issue management in the past 18 months (as of this writing—May, 1983). They include *Dun's Business Month, Chemical Week, Industry Week, The Wall Street Journal, The Management Review, Money Magazine, USA-Today, Advertising Age,* and others. Most of these have emphasized the importance of the Issue Management Process Model as a guide to new career opportunities. *Corporate Public Issues and Their Management,* by the end of 1983, had published, on a twice-monthly basis, 201 separate editions, with its readership starting at a few hundred in 1976, growing to several thousand by 1983. Issue Action Publications, publisher of CPI, and of this book, has and will make a significant contribution to the profession by devoting its entire operations to publishing issue management literature.

Each of these has had the effect of a stone dropped into a no-longer calm pool. Small ripples have become major waves. The Letters Editor of *Money Magazine,* which printed an issue management feature in March, 1983, said that no other single article stimulated so much mail. It brought hundreds of requests for more information.

The Public Affairs Handbook, published by the American Management Associations in early 1982, contained 131 direct or derivative references to the importance of issue management. Separate chapters, notably one by Robert M. Schaeberle, chairman and chief executive officer of Nabisco Brands, Inc., provided a detailed description of the integration of the issue management process into public policy management.

One chapter of *The Public Affairs Handbook* was devoted to a critique of issue management, thereby calling even more attention to the process. The critical author, nevertheless, wryly admit-

Publications on Issues Management

ted that the title and function were probably here to stay. In any event, the article added fuel to the fire of public interest in this new and challenging career potential.

The Wall Street Journal, on August 25, 1981, in its weekly front page column on Labor, precipitated the normal American tendency for like-minded people to form something. Its caption was simple: "ISSUE MANAGERS: More concerns seek top advice on coming trends." The article mentioned three names: Raymond Ewing, issues manager for Allstate; Margaret Stroup, with a similar assignment at Monsanto; and this writer—not as an editor, but as the earliest executive placement recruiter and seminar leader in the field.

Within two weeks, the three of us had received more than 250 letters and calls from every part of the country. Their common denominator was, "This is what we want to do. How do we go about it?"

Formation of The Issues Management Association

Ray Ewing and I invited ten issue management pioneers to a Harvard Club lunch in New York in December, 1981, and the Issues Management Association was born. Its original statement of mission, now incorporated into By-Laws, follows:

(1) To serve as a national and international association to encourage the development and exchange of state-of-the-art theory and practice in issues management;

(2) To assist individuals and organizations in the integration of issue management skills and objectives into management practice and decision-making;

(3) To bridge the gap between the management of issues and organizational strategic planning;

(4) To build and strengthen networks of practicing issues managers and organizations, and

to bring them case histories and examples of issues management at work;

(5) To achieve a common sense of identity among professional issues managers;

(6) To identify the related disciplines and issues which are integral components in formation of public policy, thus avoiding a fractionalized approach to public policy formation.

The fledgling organization scheduled its first membership meeting at the Library of Congress in March, 1982, thanks to the cooperation of Walter Hahn, then a major officer of the Congressional Research Service. We expected as many as 40 members, and worried about spreading them out in a room that would hold 90. However, after the room was filled, 50 more people, each with membership check in hand, had to be turned away for lack of space.

IMA's second meeting took place in November, 1982, at the headquarters of the American Management Associations in New York. This time the auditorium would hold 200, and the facilities were over-loaded. In short, the issue management process was capturing attention.

The third national meeting had George Washington University as its host in May, 1983, with Ray Ewing as chairman and Walter Hahn as program chairman. Its theme: "Issues Management and Foresight—A Private/Public Nexus."

CPI's Conference Coverage

The Spring 1983 Issues Management Association Conference, held at George Washington University in Washington, D.C. in May, attracted over 200 people or nearly half of the IMA's membership.

Foresight in Congress

Representative Albert Gore, Jr. (D-Tenn.) keynoted the first session: "We must make concerted efforts to extend Congressional outlook beyond the end of the budget year, or the next election." Gore announced his introduction that day of HR 3070, a bill to create an Office of Critical Trend Analysis in the Executive Office of the President. Designed to provide continuous assessment of trends which impact national public policy, the office would present a comprehensive report to the President in the middle of each four-year term.

Gore also mentioned the Global Foresight Roundtable of Washington, D.C., a public/private sector futuristic networking group. The Roundtable members convene every two months for a panel discussion on a topical issue. These meetings provide an opportunity for congressional staff members and Roundtable participants to talk. Gore invited private sector issues managers to attend the discussions.

"The Grand Old Lady of Issues Management"

Margaret Stroup, newly-promoted Director of Strategic Issues Analysis at Monsanto (at the advanced age of 40, introduced as the "Grand Old Lady" of issues management), once again brilliantly represented the evolution of issues management in the private sector. Stroup said that, "In 1982, Monsanto entered the third stage, and there may be more, of issues management." The Stage III phase Stroup describes as "strategic management," Stages I and II being "corporate social responsibility," and "public affairs," respectively. Monsanto managers are now asked to include 10-year strategic assumptions in their plans. Appropriations of capital distribution are based in part on these identified emerging issues.

"So what?" Stroup asked, and then answered: "The results of integration of issues management into formal planning include:

(1) Individual managers show increased sensitivity to forces that impact the bottom-line.

(2) The planning process is better. Better questions are raised. Planners are careful to include important assumptions—are more aware of their *total* environment.

(3) Monsanto responds better to the external world because it concerns itself with long term trends, as viewed by *all* stakeholders. Because of the improved view of the total picture, Monsanto is rarely in disharmony with society.

(4) Finally, issue identification is now at the very top of the organization. The Emerging Issues Committee consists of the Chief Operating Officer, three Executive Vice Presidents, five Vice Presidents, and myself as liaison. The committee has the credibility and clout to focus on the issues of 1990."

Public Sector Use of Issue Management

The foresight function of the Federal government is educational, according to Jack Clough, staff member of the House Committee on Energy and Commerce. The Federal government ought to take issue management information and play "what-if" games, in order for issues to be discussed *before* reaching the crisis of legislation. Such foresight would stimulate political debate about future scenarios. The players would analyze these scenarios and take appropriate action.

Workshop Sessions: Issue Specific

Jerry Silverman, president of Issues Management, Inc., led a workshop (one of a concurrently held series) on issues management in developing countries. He stated flatly—though not without disagreement from other participants—that most current non-financial analysis in developing countries is macro-political risk assessment that does not examine the local capacity to carry out a business commitment. He favors "disaggregating" the social, economic, and political factors that affect business decisions, and used a "problem identification tree" as a method to identify a standard set of relevant factors. In the short time available, most of these factors could not be identified, but the discussion did reveal some of the directions issues managers must take.

CPI Comment

Although many of the sessions were general, jewels of issue information made the conference worth its registration fee. With competitive issue management experts "breeding like rabbits," the Issues Management Association faces the necessity to explore constantly widening horizons. As with many professional organizations, there can be no resting on the oars for IMA.

"Issue Management— The Bottom Line Connection"

The theme for the Fall 1983 IMA Conference demonstrated no intention of resting on the oars. Entitled "Issue Management—The Bottom Line Connection," and with Frank Connor, American Can's President as keynoter, (see Chapter 12) the program committee set forth the following Conference goals:

- "To show how issue management is a holistic or system process integrated into virtually all functions of an organization,
- "To illustrate the quantifying tools needed by issue managers to communicate with various parts of a corporate organization in terms of bottom line or profit/loss implications,
- "To present case studies of issue linkage to the

bottom line in dealing with a number of significant issues."[1]

It is fascinating to watch this new management profession, not yet ten years old, stake out its claim upon a preserve dominated by line or profit-center managers—actual responsibility for profit production and maintenance through sound public policy. It is one thing to emphasize foresight, as the Spring 1983 IMA Conference did; it is far more significant to demonstrate an action role in the manufacture of profit.

Stockholders and Board members, take notice!

Two Steps Forward— One Step Back

This brief summary (cursory though it may be) of the rising tide of public and organizational attention to issue/policy management, bids well for the future of the field and for those in it. As is probably the case in all movements, occasionally for each two steps forward, someone takes a step back. We reported earlier that late in 1982, Pepsico management decided that issue management, as such, was not germane to profit-center management, and released one of the genuinely competent people in the field. This also happened at Texaco. In early May of 1983, R.J. Reynolds, in a move described in *CPI* (May 15, 1983) under the caption, "R.J. Reynolds Shoots its Foot," went through the same desolate exercise, releasing three talented specialists. It is a pleasure to say that each of these men and women went on to more rewarding assignments.

In 1976, issue/policy management was only a theoretical name for undefined disciplines. By 1983, the organization bearing its name, The

---

[1]Prepared by Joseph Kenner, program chairman, and professor, Management Decision Laboratory, Graduate School of Business, New York University.

Issues Management Association, had 550 members in less than two years of existence. Since this could not have been predicted in 1976, it will take a brave forecaster to envision the importance of the profession by 1990.

The Future Has Arrived

CHAPTER TWELVE

The Station Platform Validation Syndrome

"The important issues don't just fade away. But those who don't manage them, do."

—*Frank J. Connor, President*
American Can Company

In the early 1950s, when executive application of the computer to corporate affairs was at about the same stage as current application of issue/policy theory and disciplines to systems management, the story is told of two chief executive officers boarding their commuter train at Rye, New York. As they settled into the easy chairs on their private car (this was "the good old days"), before the porter could bring the *Times*, *The Wall Street Journal*, and coffee—all this just before the shoe shine—Joe turned to Henry and said casually, "By the way, we bought our first computer yesterday."

Henry, impressed despite his attempts to conceal it, asked about costs, brand, installation procedures, and turned to other subjects. But not for long.

As soon as he reached his own domain, Henry called for an immediate meeting of his senior management committee. "That S.O.B. Joe has just bought a computer. Get one in here, QUICK!"

However apocryphal, the story does reveal the impact of "station platform validation" or peer pressure, on executives, or anyone else, in the decision-making process. Long memories (at least 30 years) will recall that during the 1950s, most companies with computers used less than 10 percent of their total capacity, confining them primarily to invoices, billing and other procedures now regarded as primitive in the exotic systems world of modern computers. At one company, Consumers Power, the executive validation for purchase of a computer was that it would reduce the size of the clerical force. Five years after installation, that force had more than doubled.

The analogy between corporate use of the computer and integration of issue/policy management into the executive structure continues: It took 10 years or so before senior management even began to learn how to maximize their computer investments—a process that continues 30 years later.

The issue management process, invented only 10 years ago, is in the same evolutionary stages. For example, in the early computer days, the senior managers found that they couldn't even communicate with the long-haired, be-sandalled whiz kids they found in their own air-conditioned computer headquarters—the frequently undisciplined and irreverent youngsters who made the computers tick. FORTRAN and COBOL and binary process?

Today a similar condition prevails insofar as issue management talent is concerned. Hundreds of major companies have down-the-line employees, fascinated by applications of discipline to public policy management.

Earlier chapters have indicated the origins of issue management literature. Even its professional attackers—guarding their own "territorial imperatives"—have added to the groundswell of executive interest.

"Don't Bother Us"

One more reference to the analogy between corporate computer growth and adaptation to issue management: Thirty years ago, the fear of automation as a result of computerization was the hallmark of learned academicians, labor leaders, and thousands of highly publicized "view-with-alarmers." As in the case of Consumers Power, subsequent developments have shown the complainers to be false prophets.

Like Canute defying the tide, the agitators against integration of new disciplines into archaic management structures have the same complaints. "Issue management is manipulative." "Issue management will destroy the carefully built chemical relationships between the traditional public affairs executive and the boss." "Issue management destroys the professional distinctions between executives labelled corporate strategists, or risk analysts, or government and public relations directors." "Issue management is just another name for what we have always been doing." "Issues can't be managed."

In short, don't bother us.

The Tide Rolls On

Examples of integration of issue/policy management disciplines into corporate governance are illustrative. In 1976, **International Paper,** under the redoubtable leadership of Stanley Smith, took "the company issue position to the field—to all plant, sales, and marketing office locations." The total management intent was "to explain the company's position to its employees, its community leaders, and to state and nationally elected representatives.... Their (employees) should understand that their effectiveness in these activities will be measured in their annual performance and review evaluations" (the carrot *and* the stick).

Robert Dee, as president and CEO of **Smith-Kline Corporation,** as early as 1976, instituted his famous series of "Issues for Action" publications featuring such subjects as **(1)** "Government Regulation: A Growing Threat to the Public Interest;" **(2)** "Polls, Paradoxes, Pendulums and People;" **(3)** "Government Spending and Political Freedom;" **(4)** "Government Spending and the Popular Conscience."

Also in 1976, William S. Mitchell, president of **Safeway Stores,** having done his issue identification and analysis homework, moved into issue action programming by telling his stockholders and employees that "the $130 billion spent annually by business and private taxpayers for record-keeping, report filing and compliance with frequently contradictory government regulations would be enough to feed every man, woman and child in America, with several billions back for change." This added fuel to the future President Reagan's vow to deregulate.

IBM, faced in 1974 more than any other company with the issue of personal privacy, adopted the dynamic mode of issue action by establishing the following principles governing employee privacy:

(1) "Individuals should have access to information about themselves in record-keeping systems....

(2) "There should be some way for an individual to amend an inaccurate record.

(3) "An individual should be able to prevent information from being improperly disclosed or used for other than authorized purposes without his consent, unless required by law.

(4) "The custodian of data files containing sensitive information should take reasonable precautions to be sure that the data are reliable and not misused."

In 1976, President Carter appointed the first **White House** issue manager, by that title, Stuart Eisenstadt.

In 1977, **Shell Oil,** under the talented leadership of F.W. Steckmest, maintained a working Issue File and an Issue Source Book covering about 60 issues of high priority importance to the company.

In 1977, Richard B. Scudder, former publisher of the Newark (NJ) *Evening News,* founder of the **Garden State Paper Company** (now a subsidiary of Media General, Inc.) and pioneer in the paper recycling movement, was faced with a threat from the Hackensack Meadowlands Commission. It proposed building the world's largest incinerator a few miles from the Scudder recycling plant to burn waste paper, thereby threatening the entire newsprint recycling movement. Scudder opted for issue management. After identifying, analyzing, and placing priorities on the urgent issue of source of supply, the Garden State Paper Company wrapped itself in the environmental mantle of the recycling cause and eliminated the danger.

In 1977, **General Motors,** whose then chairman was T.A. Murphy, recognized the validity of the issue of employee unrest. Using Task Forces, the company acknowledged the high priority of the quality of life movement and surveyed: **(1)** An evaluation of specific quality of work life improvement efforts; **(2)** Measurement of the impact of management actions and organizational changes on quality of work life; and **(3)** Early signals of potential employee problems in order that "constructive action can be taken." Along with its major profit center reorganization in January, 1984, the company is now studying the issue management process of other major companies.

In 1978, Kalman B. Druck, the chairman of the Executive Committee, **Harshe-Rotman & Druck,** forecast that "Public relations professionals will combine a number of current concepts and techniques into 'Issue management'—making 'public issue impact centers' as important as profit centers."

The National Bank of Detroit, responding to the factual accuracy of a *New York Times* report that Detroit "is the first large dead city in the nation," organized a major issue action program (in 1977) to restore some sense of justice and order to Detroit, to the unanimous applause of every segment of the city.

In 1978, **Milton R. Wessell** published his book, *Rule of Reason,* describing the issue management process whereby determined environmentalists and equally determined industrialists developed guidelines for the orderly and acceptable use of coal. As stated earlier, these usually adversarial groups actually agreed on more than 200 steps the nation can take to use its coal reserves to the optimum advantage of both public and private interests.

Passage of intervening years has geometrically multiplied these examples of integration of issue management principles and disciplines into private sector management structures. Recent examples of CEO leadership in issue management follow:

W.H. Krome George, as chairman and CEO of Aluminum Company of America, and Robert M. Schaeberle, as chairman and CEO of Nabisco Brands, supply two classic examples of the need for, and integration of, issue management into senior executive structures, in respective chapters in *The Public Affairs Handbook* (AMACOM, 1982).

W.H. Krome George: Aluminum Company of America

George describes the inevitability of a "new management" principle: The demands of the CEO "and the implications for the organization require new kinds of training for career planning in business management." Superior persons are required "with a breadth similar to that of the CEO in key spots." This clarion call for a "new breed" of management, to be found in the issue management calling precedes by a chapter or two Robert M. Schaeberle's detailed analysis on how "Nabisco Brands follows an internal procedure of issues management."

"We attempt," Schaeberle writes, "to apply quantitative analysis and modern management principles to a function that used to be conducted on an *ad hoc* and even seat-of-the-pants basis. The process has four steps: issue identification, issue analysis, corporate position development, and articulation."

Robert M. Schaeberle: Nabisco Brands

After describing each of these stages of the Issue Management Process Model, found in this book, Nabisco's chairman furnished examples of high priority issues to which he and his colleagues apply the issue management system. "On the legislative side, the issue of truck deregulation, railroad revitalization, Conrail, and sodium labelling have been addressed. On the regulatory side, the issues of food labelling, polychlorinated biphenyls (PCBs), chlorofluorocarbons (CFCs), and sodium labelling have been subject to the issue management process."

Profit consequences? "Proper resolution of these issues," he concludes, "resulted in millions of dollars of savings to Nabisco Brands. Moreover, both the corporation and the nation benefit from improved public policy decisions, which result from the application of management decision-making techniques to complex public issues."

As the lawyer says, "The defense rests." As the issue manager says, "The best defense is a good offense."

Francis J. Connor: American Can

But the explosive growth of application of issue/policy management within corporations continues apace. Executive propensity to think of and discuss issue/policy management merely as theory is rapidly disappearing. On May 11, 1983, Francis J. Connor, president of American Can, addressed the annual conference of the North American Society for Corporate Planning on the causative factors of that company's restructuring decisions. American Can's senior management, with Board approval, combined strategic planning, the issue process, and risk assessment to achieve what *The Wall Street Journal* has described as "the most dramatic restructuring in American corporate history."

On November 7, 1983, speaking before the Issues Management Association, Connor was even more specific. "The time available for making decisions is growing shorter and shorter, and the stakes bigger and bigger. Technological, economic, and social changes are happening ever faster. And a company can no longer comfort itself that 10 or 11 digits worth of assets will carry it through. The railroads thought that, Detroit thought it, so did the textiles and rubber and shipbuilding and steel and retailing industries."

As a result of shift from micro- to macro-economics in a global world, which at American Can created an "evolution from tissues to issues," the company, he said, turned to process management of issues, policy, and strategic planning "to generate an atmosphere that seemed to *breed*...the adaptability" to redefine and change itself.

Connor's description of transforming theory into executive practice is worth noting. "We have a corporate planning office, consisting of our chairman, senior executives, and several professional strategic planners. They monitor day-to-day developments in the economy at large. They identify, in broad outline, issues that seem likely to affect our business. They bring those issues to the attention of our business-unit executives: ' What are the implications of such-and-such for your business?' It works the other way, too, the business units alerting the corporate office to issues *they* perceive.... A give and take follows: information, projections, and then recommended responses, flow between staff and line.[1] Amplifications may be needed, a more probing evaluation may be indicated, demands for a bolder projection

---

[1] See Chapter 14 for suggested corporate organization that makes "the flow between staff and line" possible and required between two senior officers—the Executive Vice President, Policy, and the Executive Vice President, Operations.

may arise. The dialogue goes on continually; only the issues change."

Connor added that for his company, "the whole train of events—the antitrust action of 30 years ago, American Can's early diversification strategy, the changed economy, and the decline of the basic industries, our new strategy and the restructuring of the company—all of that was the direct stepwise result of public issues...and the will to act upon them."

Jerry D. Geist: Public Service Company of New Mexico

At the same conference, Jerry D. Geist, president and CEO of Public Service Company of New Mexico, freely discussed the role of issue management from the perspective of a company with major changes in its strategy, including diversification, the unique challenges facing a heavily regulated industry, and issue management as a tool in decision-making and strategy formulation. He, too, along with Connor, emphasized the importance of organizational awareness of the issue management function and its integration into both line and staff operations.

Rafael D. Pagan: Nestlé Coordination Center for Nutrition

Dr. Rafael D. Pagan, Jr., president of Nestlé Coordination Center for Nutrition, also at the IMA conference, provided a specific case history on issue management's "integration into both line and staff operations." Nestlé faced, in Pagan's words, "the most pervasive, vicious, scurrilous and morale-wrecking attacks in modern times against one of the world's largest and most prestigious corporations." The issue, of course, was infant feeding.

Pagan described the milieu in which he was asked to accept senior management responsibility. "First, we are asked to make issue management and its long-term perspective compatible with corporate goals while our senior managements are frequently operating under demands for short-term return on investments, time-tables, and goals.

"Second, we must integrate the issue and issue management process with other corporate functions, and with the whole of corporate operations and structure—no minor task."

Nestlé senior management, both in this country and in Switzerland, agreed to five stipulations listed by Dr. Pagan before he would accept his issue management responsibility:

(1) "We would deal with the issue—not the activist critics.

(2) "We would receive full support and authority from the highest levels of corporate management.

(3) "Some dramatic measures were required in our relations with the various publics. Changes in policy would be required.

(4) "Management at all levels would be involved as active participants in the strategy.

(5) "Development of a strategy and conduct of operation in that strategy would be handled by a Nestlé group—a new company specially tailored with expertise in food, science and nutrition as well as in the political and sociological disciplines."

Wayne C. Anderson, vice president, government relations, at Nabisco Brands described his company's issue action response to the sodium labelling issue. Even though not under the "vicious, scurrilous, and morale-wrecking attacks" that Nestlé suffered, Nabisco Brands clearly recognized the rising public consciousness about potential health risks in product sodium content. Anderson brought in a group of scientists and government affairs representatives to define, analyze, and place priority on the sodium issue.

After all parties had agreed that sodium was a major public policy problem, the company formed

The Sodium Labelling Issue

a task force to create the issue action program. Its members were drawn from marketing, manufacturing, food scientists, and government relations professionals. After intensive discussion, the task force selected the strategy of endorsing voluntary labelling of selected products, in a manner the company felt most clearly communicated necessary information to consumers.

One by-product of Nabisco Brands' issue/policy management in this sensitive area, says Anderson, "is the support and responsiveness of FDA on this issue."

The Emerging Pattern

With private sector leadership increasingly accepting the issue/policy management theory, and—more important—demonstrating how, as Schaeberle, Geist, Connor, Pagan, and Anderson say, its results can be translated into the multi-millions of savings or profit, it is still only realistic to admit that there remain large pockets of executive skepticism and simple lack of knowledge about issue management and its implications to executive promotion. CEOs are traditionally appointed from the ranks of profit center management, or from marketing, finance, and sometimes law. Will the time come when demonstrated competence in issue/policy management is the determining factor in elevation to chief executive officership?

The point seems worth examining, and under the caption below, the following paragraphs are adapted from *CPI* for November 1, 1983.

"Issue Management and CEO Selection"

The average CEO occupancy of that high office is about six years. Statistically then, the passage of any single year will see Boards of Directors' selection of new CEOs in a little less than 17 percent of companies. That means that about 165-170 CEOs of the 1,000 largest companies are replaced, for whatever cause, each year, or about 330-340 in the 2,000 largest companies. Sic transit gloria mundi!

These calculations prompt some musings about the sources of CEO replacement. Historically, the pendulum of succession has swung back and forth from operations, finance, marketing, or law, depending on the experience and profit contribution of the contending candidates.

This rule of thumb, however, derives—if not from gentler times—from the traditional theory that profit production in the free and open marketplace is the prime arena in which the new CEO will display his or her wares. The role of government in earlier "halcyon" days was that of benevolent and pliable advocate, protector, and

tolerant chaperone for almost any business practice, ethical or not by modern standards, that
didn't totally outrage Congress. And Congress
itself was often heavily influenced by corporate
powers, and thus not easily outraged.

But today even the strongest diehards—*especially* the strongest diehards—agree that vast
changes have occurred. (And they hate all of
them!)

Question: If the dimensions of tomorrow's CEO
are so vastly different from yesterday's, if mastery
of production, marketing, or finance is no longer
adequate preparation for chief executive officership, what then are the new dimensions?

The answer, fundamentally, is easy. The new
CEO, as Krome George says, must have the depth
and breadth to recognize that ability to manage
public issues and to participate in creation of
public policies, rather than be their catspaw, is
today's long-run requirement for the CEO candidate.

To recognize all this theory is not enough. Any
Board of Directors must assure itself that its
candidate gives more than lip service to the social,
economic, and political agility required by modern
times; the candidate must have some knowledge
and experience in the issue/policy management
disciplines.

The Board Dilemma: How can a Board choose
wisely between the best of the traditionalist, and
the best of the issue/policy managers? What is to
be made of the corporate future if Board members
themselves apply only the outdated standards of
profit creation, important as it remains, through
production, marketing, or finance, and ignore the
complex and adversarial world of interrelationships in which the company must now survive?

The buck is about to stop squarely at the Board room. The newly selected CEO is not to be faulted for inadequacy in issue/policy management, if indeed the Board is equally inadequate.

Following this logic, it is apparent that the 15,000 to 20,000 Directors of America's 1,000 largest companies, and the 165 to 170 new CEOs about to replace their predecessors each year in the same companies, share a responsibility far larger than managing this quarter's return on investment. They must find in one and the same person the capacities to manage both profit and public policy. Either without the other is the road to corporate ruin.

The conviction just expressed reveals a far different universe than once prevailed. As far back as February 1, 1979, captioned "*CPI* and the Winds of Change—A New Policy," this author noted: "Perhaps out of old loyalties, we have believed until recently that the CEO would turn to the public affairs or public relations officer to fill the new high offices.... However, beginning now ...major editorial attention will be addressed directly to CEOs, high officers in public policy, to the corporate strategists, and to the corporate external relations officer.... In short, *CPI* is for those who call the shots in places where the buck stops."

But in 1979 our sights were too low. The buck does not stop with the CEOs near the end of their six-year executive generation. It stops with their successors and with the Boards that appoint them.

CHAPTER THIRTEEN

The Inevitable Corporate Reorganization

"Something which has never before been done cannot be done except by methods which have never before been tried."

—*Anonymous*

We have already spoken of the difficulties and disadvantages of trying to put square pegs in round holes. Traditional pyramidal corporate organization charts are rarely projections of change-management. They tend, instead, to become granite monuments to past practices, or a Berlin Wall intended to protect offices and departments which had been created to meet earlier—and now out of date—requirements of the institution. A vice president of strategic planning, or public relations, or public affairs does not lightly accept the coming merger of all these functions into the larger arena of issue/policy management, at least unless it is likely that he or she will emerge as the dominant factor.

When IBM decided to borrow $5 billion; when Motorola had to decide whether to manufacture chips in Mexico, Taiwan, Singapore, and in Japan itself; when Ford began "world car" production with its *Escort* parts manufactured in many countries; when American Can, the world's first major container manufacturer, decided to "restructure" and move into the insurance and financial services business—each and every one of these decisions demanded full use of the four stages of issue management, which until recently had been confined to the "public" or external issue world.

It is hard to understand why it took so long to realize that the disciplines inherent in public issue management were equally vital to profit-center decision-making. Those who had added to their traditional public relations and public affairs skills the larger dimensions of *public issue management* were really serving their time as apprentices in issue management, preparing for the day when the senior corporate or institutional officers discovered that beneath their very noses a new management art and science was being created. Despite the fact that many CEOs still do not understand this, there is NO corporate issue, of any kind, to which the issue management process is not both applicable and vital.

Realization at Board and senior executive levels that this is true, will compel management to undertake an inevitable corporate reorganization.

Thus, while students and practitioners of issue/policy management were increasing numerically, the frozen architecture of the traditional corporate structure remained an obstacle to recognition of their importance. Clearly, the century old corporate organization chart demanded modernization, not for the sole purpose of accommodating the new breed but to provide corporations with the flexibility and agility to move into the 21st century.

Needless to say, this modernization process is a little like attacking a sacred icon. In pre-planning this transgression against time-honored precedent, I sent the rough draft of "The Corporate Imperative: Management of Profit *and* Policy" (to follow) and a proposed reorganization chart to ten chief executive officers, to ten eminent academicians and authors, and to ten senior corporate officers bearing the public relations or public affairs titles in major companies.

Seven of the ten CEOs responded positively, at least in theory. "You're on course," was the common denominator. Seven of the ten professors and authors in general agreed that the proposal was "on the right track," but they emphasized that the document "may be ahead of its time."

Conversely, nine of the ten "external relations" officers urged caution. "Right or not," they said, "this concept will upset the delicate chemical balances we have achieved with senior management." In other words, cease and desist. Don't rock the boat.

However "The Corporate Imperative: Management of Profit *and* Policy," with its proposed model for corporate reorganization, appeared in

CPI, for March 1, 1982. Both the chart and its rationale follow.

The Rationale

No organization chart ever made a company or a person *work*. People make charts work, sometimes by never thinking of them at all. A traditional chart has little value except as a wall decoration, or as a page in an annual report. Moreover, an antiquated or traditional chart, with inadequate or no provisions for managing societal change factors, as well as profit, can destroy morale, create executive and staff disillusion, frustrate announced corporate policies, and make even a profitable company a sitting duck for its adversaries.

Most corporate organization charts today are obsolete. They are designed to achieve performance in one single monolithic function—the manufacture of profit. All the traditional boxes connected by solid and dotted lines, representing profit center management, and the service staffs presumably on board to help the line managers, are keyed to the myth that profit is the first, foremost, and literally the *only* reason for being of capitalist institutions.

This is a costly myth, and it is time to dispel it. There is a second *prime* function of management—effective participation in formulation of public policy, rather than mere reaction to policies made by others. Public policy and profit are equal in importance. Neither is secondary to the other.

For an example, A.T.&T. is not being broken up for lack of profit or for lack of efficiency in providing products and services. It has been reshaped, for good or evil, because of its inability to participate effectively in formulating the public policy that determines its destiny. It has been the victim, the tail of the kite, of public policy made by its adversaries who overwhelmed it with legislation, judicial fiats, regulation, and public suspicion of its "undue concentration of economic power." A.T.&T.'s chairman, Charles L. Brown, has made it abundantly clear that, whatever the company's future may be, dissolution was not its choice.

On the other end of the spectrum, Chrysler—bereft of profit (then!)—remains alive *because* of its ability to influence public policy.

Yet the myth survives: Profit is the be-all and end-all of American business. Large and powerful consulting firms, with fees in the millions of dollars, concentrate their skills and energies on more effective organization for what is loosely called "strategic planning," or business strategies—the objective being increased profit. They could not exist without being undeniably effective. They earn their keep.

We propose, however, that "business strategic planning" is a buzz-phrase and a misleading prop that helps perpetuate the myth that the sole objective of management is profit.

In reality, strategic planning is two separate and discrete, but interdependent functions, with each deserving the most senior executive attention and top management skills.

The first of these twin functions is strategic profit planning. The second, equally important, is strategic policy planning.

Each has its own separate disciplines. Each must be coordinate with the other. Each demands executive commitment, talent, and budget. Each can be organizationally designed, charted and its results measured. Each is part and parcel of the control function of management. Management demeans its own profession by failure to manage policy with the same skills it applies to profit.

To demonstrate this thesis, we propose a real world corporate organization chart (see page 141). Its resemblance to all previous designs is merely

superficial. It challenges the myth that profit—
now—is the most important of all management
objectives, and suggests operational processes to
achieve an even more basic corporate objective—
survival itself. Profit is an end-product of meeting
perceived needs through production and marketing. Survival, however, is based on corporate
capacity to meet deeper needs arising from technological, social, economic, and political tidal
waves.

**A Word
of Caution**

The unique organizational chart that appears
here is not intended to be superimposed, intact,
on an operating company. It is, however, a roadmap or set of guidelines by which senior management can coordinate and execute the *two* major
responsibilities of business: strategic *profit* planning and action and strategic *policy* planning
and action.

Finally, it is a chart of functions—not of people.
Smaller companies may well have one person
occupying several of the boxes.

What follows is an explanation and rationale for
each charted function combining policy with
profit management.

**Corporate
Reorganization
for the
Real World**

Note first the two principal functions of the "new
management," as they appear in the ovals at top
left and right. The purpose of public policy management is **positive—not reactive—participation
in the formulation of public policy in order to
assure corporate survival.** The purpose of the
operational units is, in one word, **profit.**

The **Board of Directors'** function is traditional:
to determine over-all **corporate policy,** to evaluate results produced by management, and, when
necessary, to change management.

The function of the **Chief Executive Office** is to
execute policies laid down by the Board, earn a
profit, justify investors' confidence, maintain pro-

function: **Law** and **Issue Management.** As in the case of Finance, there will be enraged reactions from the corporate general counsels who are accustomed by tradition to report directly to the CEO. Yet law professionally is recognized as the summation of "the customs and mores of the people." These are precisely the causative factors of economic, political, and social change with which the Public Policy executive must be concerned. The corporate lawyer is constantly engaged in either advocating, or defending against, public policy as established in law or regulations. This allocation of the legal function to the Public Policy officer can eliminate the "Iron Curtain" that frequently separates the legal counsel from those charged with traditional external relations functions.

Further, there is no reason why the post of Public Policy officer cannot be held by the lawyer. Pragmatically, this is already happening in numerous companies, just as people trained in Finance are often named head of Operations.

The Issue Management functions must be regarded as the skilled use of tools and disciplines for achieving more effective participation in *formulating* public policy rather than merely reacting to it. The major functions of Issue Management are stated on the chart. They are: **issue identification, issue analysis, the organization and management of combined policy and profit center task forces to determine the highest priorities of policy issues,** and finally, the actual **issue action programming,** proactively, to prevent adverse public trends from overwhelming even the most profitable company (or to create new trends that combine both corporate and public good).

The issue management processes are spelled out in detail in the Issue Management Process Model. They are not like Topsy who "jes' growed."

They are logical and scientific processes to be studied and applied. They are disciplines vital to management by systems.

The four major functions reporting to the issue management executive are shown as **External Constituencies, Contributions Management, Internal Constituencies,** and **Communications and Media Relations.**

The two most important functions of External Constituencies are listed as **Federal and State Government Relations,** and **Advocacy Group Relations.** To the degree that the Reagan-sponsored "new federalism" program becomes even partially a fact of life, the capacity to undertake, affect, and act upon both Federal and state regulatory activities has enormous and burgeoning importance. Here again, the opportunity to manufacture profit, either near-term or long-term, depends in large part on the company's skill in public policy management.

The chart shows three major areas of the Internal Constituencies function: **Employees, Plant/ Community,** and **Investor Relations.** The person, or persons, with these responsibilities cannot afford to be merely responsive to these constituencies; he or she must be anticipatory and proactive, as described in the Issue Management Process Model.

The Final Surprise

The final surprise will not be a surprise at all to modern issue management practitioners, who already recognize **communications** as the ultimate stage of issue action programming. Its appearance at the bottom of this chart does not diminish its importance. The manager in charge of communications has as much opportunity to contribute to corporate public policy as any of the other issue management specialists. In addition, he or she will be expected to listen to the distant drums of public sentiment, and to command and use the entire range of communications skills on behalf of the corporate public policy to which he or she has contributed. Just as it is possible for the lawyer, or public affairs professional, the communications and media manager can earn, or perhaps has already earned, the right to be Executive Vice President—Public Policy.

Until that time comes, however, the manager of Communications and Media Relations has overwhelming responsibilities as charted. That office is the coordinated and articulated voice, as shown by the dotted lines, of all phases of both Policy and Profit management. Its responsibility not only for story placement and creative writing, but also for media research, content analysis, and above all for the "listening process"—is vital to the issue identification and analysis stages of the issue management system.

In Summary

This new and even revolutionary organizational design is intended to bring order, logic, control, effectiveness, and economy into twin major responsibilities of corporate management—profit and public policy. Neither alone can ensure survival. Integrated and managed, they have a fighting chance.

We have under-emphasized actual economies to be gained by this "new management" system. Literally countless companies are encumbered by overlapping empires or baronies, each clamoring for talent, budgets, space, and executive attention for their fractional contribution to policy and profit management, yet none with actual accountability for total and measurable results of their efforts.

It will take bold leadership to remodel existing structures in accordance with this model. Expect sabotage, foot-dragging, sand-bagging, and attempted pocket vetoes whenever and wherever the established seats of power and authority see encroachment on their empires.

To conclude: The functions of Profit and Public Policy are coordinate and equal in importance. It is the new responsibility of management to act accordingly. The more traditional organization charts ignore or underestimate the manageability of public policy. This can no longer be taken lightly. The chart will help avoid traditional mistakes.

It would be pleasant, but not factual, to report that hordes of CEOs and their Boards at once feverishly instituted the reorganization which would have created two senior officers, one for profit management and the other for policy management, each mutually interrelated by the strategic planning function. In fact, the proposed reform moves with all the speed of a glacier. But it is moving.

On May 1, 1983, *CPI* (the only publication to do so) reported on the true significance of the restructuring of the IBM Board, as follows:

"IBM's Policy Board"

On March 30, 1983, IBM became the first major company to establish a corporate board for management of *policy* and *profit.* Under John Opel's chairmanship, the IBM Board has two major committees, the Policy Committee (to establish corporate goals and be responsible for major policy issues), and the Business Operations Committee (responsible for IBM's business plans and strategies process, review, and approval of major product announcements and day-to-day operations). The new Board replaces the Corporate Office and Corporate Management Committees, which formerly were IBM's top management organizations.

Designed to enable IBM to "capitalize on growth opportunities," the new structure directs senior operating managers to regard public policy management as co-equal in importance with profit.

According to a company spokesman, "The operating executives will now run their organizations and, as well, meet on the committee wearing a corporate responsibility hat." The new structure will involve the senior management of the major IBM operating units more fully in the corporate decision process and distribute decision-making authority more broadly.

To emphasize the critical need for chief executive total *commitment,* Opel assumes chairmanship of the Policy Committee, along with John F. Akers, president, and Paul J. Rizzo, vice chairman. Senior Vice President Dean P. Phypers will be chairman of the Business Operations Committee. Thus the senior IBM Board becomes the turf where both policy and profit meet on equal terms.

CPI Comment: On the wry side, we quote the spokesman again: "The new corporate board was not the brainstorm of any one individual." He went on to say that a senior unnamed officer, had devised it. "We can't claim it's unique, but it's certainly not patterned after any other firm."

IBM's leadership will become bellwether for many other companies in elevation of policy management to top level responsibility. Let one major company pioneer a breakthrough, and dozens follow, lamenting all the while that they hadn't moved first.

Between March of 1982 and 1984, fifty or so more corporations have created Board-level committees on Issues, Policy, Corporate Social Responsibility, etc. More and more issue managers, by whatever corporate label have become the rapporteurs, or secretaries, of these multiplying Board committees. They write the agendas and summarize the conclusions. (Never underestimate the power of the agenda writer!)

Precisely as the small preview study had indicated, genuine issue/policy management, when installed at senior levels, was, in general, the "trickle-down" process at work. Senior managements and their Boards were responding to the demands of change, but not, unfortunately, to demands from the majority of managers of the traditional external relations functions.

The implications seem clear. Traditions are not immune to the force of an idea whose time has come. Either the external relations traditionalists at every level will adapt to the disciplines required for the issue/policy future, or they will be superseded by those who see the vision.

CHAPTER FOURTEEN

Issue/Policy Management as a Career Opportunity

"The wave of the future is coming
and there is no fighting it."

—*Anne Morrow Lindbergh*
The Wave of the Future *(1980)*

"Those who see the vision," the last words of the preceding chapter, are the focus of this concluding section.

The senior executive who seeks talent in the exciting new world of issue/policy management needs a reservoir from which to draw this talent.

Similarly, the aspiring issue/policy manager has no future unless and until the senior corporate officers of major companies understand that:

(a) Management science didn't stop yesterday;

(b) Issue/policy management, coupled with strategic planning and policy risk assessment, is the wave of the future;

(c) More than 500 corporations now employ issue managers; and

(d) The reservoir of available talent grows each day.

Thus, the intent of this final chapter is to assure CEOs that the talent is out there, and to assure the issue managers that someone needs and will seek their skills.

With this in mind, the catechism of questions the applicant should ask is equally relevant to the potential employer. Each needs the other. The problem is to arrange that they understand each other.

"What's In It for Me?"

The brightest idea, whether it is social, economic, political, or technological, without disciples or advocates, is a shimmering delusion. "What's in it for me?" That question probably crossed the mind of the cave man when he first experimented with fire, and it is no less relevant to the would-be issue/policy manager.

The vision itself deserves restatement: The time is coming, and indeed is here, when the sound management of institutional policy is as important as the sound management of profit. Or, in terms of the issue management process itself, the time has come to move out of the reactive and adaptive modes of response to critical issues into the proactive or dynamic modes. When one can't win against powerful adversarial forces, it is time to change the theater of war.

There are three basic requirements for a career in issue/policy management. They are as applicable to the chief executive officer as to the candidate. Use them as a check list for both corporate and self-evaluation.

Requirements for a Career in Issue Management

(1) Dissatisfaction with *status quo*;
(2) A broad educational background;
(3) A sense of personal destiny.
Each of these deserves discussion.

(a) Do traditional organizational forms meet the social, economic, political, and technological needs of the present and the future?

Dissatisfaction with Status Quo

(b) Is there a clear organizational career path for the issue manager's participation in executive decision-making?

(c) Do the line, or profit, managers acknowledge and respect the contributions of the issue/policy resource in terms of their own success and self-esteem? And vice versa?

(d) Does the company or institution have the tolerance, the machinery, and the talent, to network the persons or groups with critical, cynical, or antagonistic attitudes towards the company's functions or tactics?

(e) Does the company measure every major decision in terms of the "accelerating social, economic, and political changes" listed in Stage I of the Issue Management Process Model?

(f) Does the company or institution have chief executive commitment to solid issue action programming?

(g) Is the issue/policy management function firmly integrated into the executive decision-making process?

(h) Does senior management recognize that issue/policy management, risk assessment, and strategic planning are all interrelated, or, indeed, the same functions?

(i) Are you asked for all that you can give?

(j) Do the human resources or personnel patterns of the company or institution provide an uncluttered route to highest levels of responsibility?

(k) Is issue/policy management skill a factor in bonuses and extra compensation?

An honest negative response to any of these questions would explain dissatisfaction with *status quo* for anyone of the new breed who believes that today's companies or institutions are in the fourth managerial revolution, the elevation of Policy management to a level equal with Profit management.

Of course, there will always be reasonably rewarding careers for thousands who can live quite comfortably despite answering "no" to the questions listed. They do not choose to cause tremors in status quo. Permanent assignment to a staff level position does not trouble them. But this is a book about management revolution, and, as we said in Chapter One, one can't scramble an egg without first breaking the shell. This is a book for men and women who *do* intend to rock the boat.

A Broad Educational Background

There is no educational discipline that is a shortcut to Rome in issue management. Benvenuto Cellini talked of "l'huomo universale." While paragons of that kind are in short supply, it can be said that for issue/policy managers, the broader and deeper the cultural, social science, people-oriented, and technology-appreciative his or her interests are, the greater the future the aspirant has.

It may be arithmetically incorrect to say that the whole is greater than the sum of the separate parts, but it is totally true for companies and institutions. Much is being written about "corporate cultures." This chimerical quality, whatever it may be, is not merely the composite of production, marketing, or financial skills. It is not merely "love of customers." Rather, it is the public perception of the totality of institutional character, a kind of effluvia that creates an identity of its own.

It is almost a truism to write that people—the ultimate arbiters of institutional destiny in a non-dictatorial society—do not react on the *facts* they *know*, but on what they *think* they *know*. In short, attitudes about the corporate culture—not its separate parts—will determine corporate survival in a pluralistic world. Attitudes either attract or repel the talent on which the future depends, a lesson as important to the CEO as to issue/policy managers.

The aspirant for issue/policy management, then, cannot be inhibited by the Aristotelian concept that something *is*. Rather, he or she must realize that what apparently *is* is always in the process of *becoming*.

In other words, the would-be issue/policy manager, at whatever levels, must be able to live comfortably with the constancy of change. Since change itself is the only immutable law, the aspirant needs a lot of history, anthropology, psychology, politics—preferably both in theory and in practice, an appreciation for the literature in which change has been reported, plus the visceral recognition that sometimes vast forces will fight to resist or postpone change.

The "boat rocker" will find resistance to change within any established institution. Progressive chairmen may find it in their Board rooms, issue managers in their bosses. Even though doomed, in the longer run, the vested interests may unite, at least temporarily, to repel the innovator. Knowledge, patience, tact, and courage are prime requisites for the issue/policy manager.

All this is preface to the supreme importance of intellectual discipline in the issue manager. Casual readers, or people who are constitutionally disposed to dispassionate observation, need not apply. The issue analyst will always be useful but will never be an issue/policy *manager,* executing issue action programs or participating in executive decision-making, unless he or she has mastered the kind of discipline inherent in the four stages of the issue management process.

For a would-be issue manager to refuse to accept disciplined process is to place himself/ herself outside the pale of systems management. The Pharisee, mentioned earlier, had nothing on the external affairs person who relies on instinct, viscera, or the "whom do you know?" philosophy that invariably breeds contempt and dislike from the advocates of the system.

In other words, that "flash of genius," however refreshing, admirable, and occasionally useful it may be, resembles the extraordinary *hors d'oeuvre*—good, but it is not the whole meal.

The meal is the Issue Management Process Model, its imitators, successors, and improved versions, plus the mastery of the social, economic, and political disciplines inherent in it.

However, once a person accepts the rules—and the disciplines—anyone can play. In my six years of teaching "Public Issue Management" to MBA candidates drawn from corporate middle managements and already at the $30,000-plus level in salary, I found that—regardless of educational background or specific corporate skills—the students were enthusiastic about assembling their own issue action files on the high priority issues confronting *their* companies. They enjoyed playing the role of the CEO in creating, authorizing, and executing issue action programming. Their issue action programs, sometimes prepared in a single week, frequently exceeded the quality of corporate in-house programs that may have taken company staffs a year to assemble.

Thus, after all these observations about academic or learning preparation for a career in issue/policy management, the real mood-music is that which anyone can play—provided that he or she has a sense of personal destiny and the discipline required to achieve it.

Apparently, one either has this sense of destiny or one does not. Frequently, it is a vital spark in a heavily banked ash heap, not bursting into flame until prodded.

A Sense of Personal Destiny

James Ford Bell, founder and CEO of General Mills, was my first corporate boss. He had transformed a grain elevator and flour milling company into a broad grocery manufacturer, with *Gold Medal Flour* and *Wheaties* as its early front-running products. I had noticed in *Who's Who in America* that Mr. Bell, then a member of the Board of A.T.&T., the Pullman Company, General Mills, and others, listed himself as a "capitalist" with a small "c." One day I asked him for his reasons, and he responded very seriously: "A capitalist is a person who tries to leave the world a little richer at the end of his life than it was at the beginning."

James Ford Bell had a sense of destiny.

If destiny is predetermined, as in Aldous Huxley's *Brave New World* or in Orwell's *1984*, where every phase of human destiny was first established and then governed by "Big Brother," there is little or no room for emergence of a sense of personal destiny. Only Big Brother manages issues—all of them.

But, in the shrinking parts of the world—where

freedom of choice, based on fundamentally held values about individual human dignity and liberty, exists—a sense of destiny, or the basic belief that "the traditional practices need changing, and I can change them," can flourish and be rewarded. The process of doing so won't be "beer and skittles." And the desired objective won't happen without this sense of destiny, aided by a system that transforms the identified issue into the desired action.

Afterthought

The earth, its sister planets, and all their moons and satellite asteroids revolved around the sun for aeons before Galileo was persecuted for "discovering" this ancient fact. Laws of gravity existed from the beginnings of time and Newton merely gave them a definition and a label. Darwin's years of meticulous observations, culminating in his *The Origins of Species*, brought process to bear on a wilderness of random theories. The Id existed in the human animal before Freud made it central to modern psychiatry. Fire existed long before primordial man first harnessed it. The principle of the wheel needed only some visionary tinkerer to "invent" it as a substitute for the sled. E equals MC² was and forever will be a fact of the universe. It took an Einstein to give it a language.

It isn't surprising that King Solomon earned his reputation for wisdom at least partially by concluding that "There is no new thing under the sun."

Issue/policy management, while less cosmic, also has its origins deep within human experience. Its separate parts, though not its totality, represent ancient knowledge. The challenge has been to convert valuable subfunctions into an orderly system of thinking about and solving real-world problems.

Other explorers will inevitably find these pages to be only an episode in the continuing evolution of a management science dedicated to *participating* in creation of policy. And they will be right.

In the meantime, however, with the help of experiential midwifery, an issue/policy management science and profession is in process of being born. It contains within itself origins of the future.

W. Howard Chase

W. Howard Chase

Bibliography

Aguilar, F.R. *Scanning the Business Environment.* New York: Macmillan, 1967.

Bloom, P.N. and Stern, L.W. "Emergence of Anti-Industrialism." *Business Horizons,* Vol. 19, No. 5, October 1976.

Boe, A.R. "Fitting the Corporation to the Future." *Public Relations Quarterly,* Vol. 24, No. 4, Winter 1979.

Brown, J.K. *This Business of Issues: Coping With the Company's Environments.* New York: Conference Board, 1979.

Buchholz, R.A. "Education for Public Issues Management: Insights From a Survey of Top Practitioners." *Public Affairs Review,* Vol. 3, 1982.

"Capitalizing on Social Change." *Business Week,* October 29, 1979.

Carnoy, M. and Shearer, D. *Economic Democracy: The Challenge of the 1980s.* Armonk, NY: M.E. Sharpe, 1980.

Chase, W.H. "Public Issue Management: The New Science." *Public Relations Journal,* Vol. 33, No. 10, October 1977.

Chase, W.H. "Prelude to the '80s: Adjusting to a Different Business/Social Climate." *Public Relations Quarterly,* Vol. 25, No. 1, Spring 1980.

Chase, W.H. "Issues Management" in J.S. Nagelschmidt (ed.). *The Public Affairs Handbook.* New York: AMACOM, American Management Associations, 1982.

"The Corporate Imperative: Management of Profit and Policy." *Corporate Public Issues and Their Management,* Vol. VII, No. 5.

Corporate Public Issues and Their Management. Stamford, CT: Issue Action Publications.

Crane, T.Y. "Issue Management Profile: Monsanto Company." *Corporate Public Issues and Their Management,* Vol. VI, No. 22.

Ehrbar, A.F. "Backlash Against Business Advocacy." *Fortune,* Vol. 98, No. 4, August 28, 1978.

Ellis, R.J. "Improving Management Response in Turbulent Times." *Sloan Management Review,* Winter 1982.

Ewing, R.P. "Advocacy Advertising: The Voice of Business in Public Policy Debate." *Public Affairs Review,* Vol. 3, 1982.

Ewing, R.P. "Modeling the Process" in J.S. Nagelschmidt (ed.). *The Public Affairs Handbook.* New York: AMACOM, American Management Associations, 1982.

Ewing, R.P. "Uses of Futurist Techniques in Issues Management." *Public Relations Quarterly,* Vol. 24, No. 4, Winter, 1979.

Fine, S.H. *The Marketing of Ideas and Social Issues.* New York: Praeger, 1981.

Fleming, J.E. "Linking Public Affairs with Corporate Planning." *California Management Review,* Vol. 23, No. 2, Winter 1980.

Fox, J.F. "Communicating on Public Issues: A Changing Role for the CEO." *Public Relations Quarterly,* Vol. 27, No. 2, Summer 1982.

The Future Agenda. Washington, D.C.: Congressional Clearing House on the Future and the Congressional Institute for the Future, November 1982.

Goldman, E. "On the Growing Need for Businesses to Take Arms Against a Sea of Initiative Troubles." *Public Affairs Review,* Vol. 3, 1982.

Gollner, A.B. *Social Change and Corporate Strategy: The Expanding Role of Public Affairs.* Stamford, CT: Issue Action Publications, 1983.

Gottschalk, E.C. Jr. "Firms Hiring New Type of Manager to Study Issues, Emerging Troubles." *Wall Street Journal,* June 10, 1982.

Hart, A.S. "Identifying Issues" in J.S. Nagel-schmidt (ed.). *The Public Affairs Handbook.* New York: AMACOM, American Management Associations, 1982.

"How to Conduct an Issue Management Seminar." *Corporate Public Issues and Their Management,* Vol. V, No. 14.

"IBM's Policy Board." *Corporate Public Issues and Their Management,* Vol. VII, No. 9.

Issue Management Letter. Alexandria, VA: Conference on Media and Issues.

"Issues Management: Far From Being a Fad." *Impact,* May 1982.

Johnson, Jon. "Issues Management: What are the Issues?" *Business Quarterly,* Fall, 1983.

Keegan, W. J. "Scanning the International Business Environment: A Study of the Information Acquisition Process." Unpublished Dissertation, Harvard University, 1967.

Kefalas, A.G. "Scanning the External Business Environment." Unpublished Dissertation, University of Iowa, 1971.

Kefalas, A.G. and Schoderbek, P.P. "Scanning the Business Environment—Some Empirical Results." *Decision Sciences,* Vol. 4, No. 1, January 1973.

Ladd, E.D. "How to Tame the Special-Interest Groups." *Fortune,* Vol. 102, No. 8, October 20, 1980.

Lesly, P. "Functioning in the New Human Climate." *Management Review,* Vol. 70, No. 12, December 1981.

McConnell, D. "Emerging Situations Surveillance and Corporate Issues Management." Working Paper, College of Business, University of Maine, September 1983.

Naisbitt, J. *Megatrends: Ten New Directions Transforming Our Lives.* New York: Warner, 1982.

National Conference of State Legislatures. "Legislative Handbook on Science and Technology Issues." Denver, CO: National Conference of State Legislatures, 1981.

Nishi, K., Schoderbeck, C. and Schoderbek, P.P. "Scanning the Organizational Environment: Some Empirical Results." *Human Systems Performance*, December 1982.

O'Toole, P. "Finding Work in Glutted Fields." *Money*, Vol. 12, No. 3, March 1983.

Paul, K. "Business Environment/Public Policy Problems for the 1980s." *Business & Society*, Winter/Spring 1981/2.

Paluszek, J.L. *Will the Corporation Survive?* Reston, VA: Reston Publishing, 1977.

Perham, J. "New Company Watchdog." *Dun's Business Month*, Vol. 118, No. 6, December 1981.

Preston, L. (ed.). *Research in Corporate Social Performance and Policy*, Vols. 1 and 2. Greenwich, CT: JAI Press, 1978 and 1980.

Regan, P.J. "The Importance of Social and Political Trends." *Financial Analysis Journal*, November/December, 1981.

Reich, R.B. "Regulation by Confrontation or Negotiation?" *Harvard Business Review*, May/June 1981.

Renfro, W.L. "Forecasting Issues" in J.S. Nagelschmidt (ed.). *The Public Affairs Handbook*. New York: AMACOM, American Management Associations, 1982.

Renfro, W.L. "Issues Management: The Changing Corporate Role." Zurich, Switzerland: Gottlieb Dutweiler Institute, October, 1982.

Roeser, T.F. "Identifying Public Affairs Resources." *Business and Society*, Winter/Spring 1981/2.

"Scouting the Future for Danger." *USA Today*, May 23, 1983.

Schaeberle, R.M. "The State of Public Affairs" in J.S. Nagelschmidt (ed.). *The Public Affairs*

Handbook. New York: AMACOM, American Management Associations, 1982.

Sethi, S.P. "Management Fiddles While Public Affairs Flops." *Business and Society Review,* No. 18, Summer 1976.

Sethi, S.P. "Business and the News Media: The Paradox of Informed Misunderstanding." *California Management Review,* Vol. 19, No. 3, Spring 1977.

Sethi, S.P. "Advocacy Advertising and the Multinational Corporation." *Columbia Journal of World Business,* Vol. 12, No. 3, Fall 1977.

Sethi, S.P. "Institutional/Image Advertising and Idea/Issue Advertising as Marketing Tools: Some Public Policy Issues." *Journal of Marketing,* Vol. 43, No. 1, January 1979.

Steiner, J.F. "Business Response to Public Distrust." *Business Horizons,* Vol. 20, No. 2, April 1977.

Thain, D.H. "Improving Competence to Deal with Politics and Government: The Management Challenge of the '80s." *Business Quarterly,* Vol. 45, No. 1, Spring 1980.

Thompson, D.B. "Issue Management: New Key to Corporate Survival." *Industry Week,* Vol. 208, No. 4, February 23, 1981.

Tisdal, C.W. "Communicating in the Doubting '80s." *Business Quarterly,* Vol. 45, No. 3, Autumn 1980.

Utterback, J.M. "Environmental Analysis and Forecasting" in D.E. Schendel and C.W. Hofer (eds.). *Strategic Management: A New View of Business Policy and Planning.* Boston, MA: Little, Brown, 1979.

Vanston, J.H. "Technical Innovation as a Strategic Issue." Austin, TX: Technology Futures Institute, December, 1982.

Vogel, D. "Ralph Naders All Over the Place." *Across the Board,* Vol. 16, No. 4, April 1979.

"Why and How of Issue Action Files." *Corporate Public Issues and Their Management,* Vol. V, No. 15.

"Why Business Got a Bad Name." *Business and Society Review,* No. 19, Fall 1976.

Williams, P.F. "Attitudes Toward the Corporation and the Evaluation of Social Data." *Journal of Business Research,* 1982.

Williamson, O.E. "The Modern Corporation: Origins, Evolution, Attributes." *Journal of Economic Literature,* Vol. 19, No. 4, December 1981.

Zenisek, T.J. "Corporate Social Responsibility: A Conceptualization Based on Organizational Literature." *Academy of Management Review,* Vol. 4, No. 3, July 1979.

Index